Decolonizing Development

This book turns to the intellectual discourses that have emerged from India and Latin America, two outposts of the Global South, on the themes of imperialism, sovereignty, development, and socio-economic, racial and caste inequalities.

It recovers the elided reflective traditions of thinkers, writers and activists from these peripheries and highlights the distinctive ideas, alliances and parallelisms in their works, as well as the manner in which they articulate liberatory paradigms that continue to have contemporary relevance. The book maps the innovative epistemic engagements of thinkers from India and Latin America, highlighting the manner in which they have disrupted and challenged the hierarchies of global knowledge production. It argues that political, spatial and historical distinctions notwithstanding, the experiences of peripheralization, their common traditions of resistance to oppression and their deeply entangled histories have forged a shared intellectual identity and a rich alternative set of emancipatory epistemologies grounded in the realities and histories of Southern nations. The book recovers this body of work as mass movements the world over seek civilizational alternatives to capitalist modernity.

The book will be of interest to students and researchers of development studies, history, political science, sociology, political economy, South Asian studies, Latin American studies and Global South studies.

Rahul A. Sirohi is Assistant Professor, Department of Humanities and Social Sciences, Indian Institute of Technology, Tirupati. He is a development economist and his research currently focuses on the development experiences of Asia and Latin America. He is the author of *From Developmentalism to Neoliberalism: A Comparative Analysis of Brazil and India* (2019) and *Reassessing the Pink Tide: Lessons From Brazil and Venezuela* (2021).

Sonya Surabhi Gupta is Professor of Latin American Studies at Jamia Millia Islamia, New Delhi. Her research interests focus on knowledge flows in the Global South, with special reference to Latin America and India in a cross-cultural context. Her most recent publication is the edited volume, *Subalternities in India and Latin America: Dalit Autobiographies and the Testimonio* (2022).

Decolonizing Development

Liberatory Epistemologies
from India and Latin America

**Rahul A. Sirohi and
Sonya Surabhi Gupta**

Routledge
Taylor & Francis Group

LONDON AND NEW YORK

First published 2024
by Routledge
4 Park Square, Milton Park, Abingdon, Oxon OX14 4RN

and by Routledge
605 Third Avenue, New York, NY 10158

Routledge is an imprint of the Taylor & Francis Group, an informa business

British Library Cataloguing-in-Publication Data
A catalogue record for this book is available from the British Library

ISBN: 978-1-032-15935-5 (hbk)
ISBN: 978-1-032-32660-3 (pbk)
ISBN: 978-1-003-31608-4 (ebk)

DOI: 10.4324/9781003316084

Typeset in Times New Roman
by Apex CoVantage, LLC

Contents

Acknowledgements

Chapter 2 of this book draws on our previously published paper titled "The Political Economy of Race and Caste: Revisiting the Writings of Mariátegui and Ambedkar" which appeared in the *Journal of Labour and Society*, Volume 23, Issue 3, in 2020 (Brill). We thank the editor and publisher for allowing us to use the paper in this book.

We acknowledge our gratitude to Natarang Pratishthan for very generously letting us consult their archival material on the 1956 Asian Writers' Conference.

Our thanks to Miguel Ángel Asturias Amado, son of Nobel Laureate Miguel Ángel Asturias, for very generously giving us his authorization for the photograph of his father in Chapter 3. Our thanks are also due to Paula Canal of the Indent Literary Agency, New York, for having given us permission to cite the poem "Problemas del subdesarrollo" of the Cuban poet Nicolás Guillén in Chapter 3.

We acknowledge with gratitude the comments and suggestions of the anonymous reviewers. Our heartfelt thanks to our editor, Shoma Choudhury from Routledge, for having guided us through the publication of this book.

Introduction

Recent events that have followed the outbreak of the Corona pandemic not only have exposed the deep-rooted flaws in global trade and global financial architecture arduously built up over the past four decades but have also laid bare the civilizational fault lines of our times. For years, advocates of neoliberalism have insisted that free trade between nations would lift all boats. The globalization of trade and finance was supposed to free up economies from the state's stranglehold and enhance access to technologies and capital on a scale that they could never have dreamed of earlier. State-interventionist strategies, it was argued from this perspective, placed too little emphasis on comparative advantage and thus ended up allocating resources in a manner that was prejudicial to efficiency and growth.[1] The virulent pandemic that began in China in late 2019 and spread across the world shortly thereafter has, however, exposed the vulnerabilities of the neoliberal project (Nelson 2020). Global growth rates have fallen, and even the most dynamic centres of the world economy are in shambles. The neoliberal folklore of the benefits of unrestricted and free trade amongst nations, which have formed the basis upon which the post-1980 world economy has been built, were challenged by the severe breakdown of global value chains of basic essential goods like masks, gloves and even life-saving medicines (Gereffi 2020). Added to this, the weakening of public health systems and the retreat of the state from social priorities, as well as the large-scale precarity of workers that have accompanied neoliberal globalization, all came back to bite even the most powerful economies in the world, which are still struggling to cope with the after-effects of the pandemic (Montes 2020). Not only have the past couple of years indicated how vulnerable global trade architecture is to supply disruptions, but they have also blasted the myths of neoliberalism regarding the superiority of market-based decision-making as governments and policymakers around the world had to adopt extreme forms of interventions that were both unprecedented and unorthodox.

What the pandemic has also done is to bring to the fore the terrible inequalities that mark modern-day capitalism. One of the founding myths of neoliberalism is its promise of equitable development. When the pandemic began, inequalities within countries and the divergences in standards of living,

DOI: 10.4324/9781003316084-1

wages and per capita incomes across the North and the South were already very visible. The pandemic only worsened these fissures and fault lines. Estimates suggest that the long-term economic costs of the pandemic will be far more severe for the developing world than for their rich country counterparts (Filippini and Yeyati 2022). Moreover, mounting external debt and the ever-present risks of capital flight have forced governments, especially in the South, into a tight corner, and the developing world has, as a result, lagged behind the developed world in extending safety nets to those that need them the most (Ghosh 2020; Jomo and Chowdhury 2020). The poorest and most socially marginalized have disproportionately suffered (Kesar *et al.,* 2021; Liebman *et al.,* 2020) and now face threats of starvation and further immiserization, reminding us once again of the centrality of class but also race, gender, ethnicity and caste in shaping the contemporary world, which stands today at the brink of a World War.

Crises such as these are pregnant with possibilities, and indeed, the multiple shocks to the neoliberal architecture combined with the pitched battles that are being waged by mass movements outside parliaments, in city squares, and in villages across the world, clearly indicate that it will not be easy to go back to business as usual now that some semblance of normalcy returns to the post-pandemic world. Neoliberalism has reached a dead end, and while the future is still far from certain, in this interregnum where the "old is dying but the new cannot be born", what is clearly needed is a new hegemonic project (Gramsci, 1971: 276). As mass struggles against neoliberalism pick up pace, conjunctures such as these require ruthless criticism of the status quo, of the manner in which our societies have been structured, and of the way in which global hierarchies have been built. And like Marx's (1887) architect who "raises his structure in imagination before he erects it in reality" what is needed more than ever are new visions for the future – visions that celebrate common aspirations shared by the insurgents of the Paris Commune, the slaves of the Haitian Uprisings, the peasants of the Moplah, Telangana Revolts and those of the Algerian and Mexican Revolution, and the masses that led the Bolshevik, Cuban and the Chinese revolutions; in short, the many insurrectionary visions that underscore our common humanity and naturally build on common experiences, but visions that at same time recognize diversity and emphasize the importance of historical and cultural conditions.

It is in this context that this book turns to the intellectual thought that emerged from India and Latin America, two outposts of the Global South, and seeks to recover the elided reflective traditions of thinkers, writers and activists from these peripheries on salient themes of imperialism, sovereignty, development and socio-economic, racial and caste inequalities in the 19th and 20th centuries. It seeks to highlight the distinctive ideas, alliances and parallelisms in their works, as well as the manner in which they articulated liberatory paradigms for the colonized and/or erstwhile colonized world. It underscores the contemporary relevance of this body of work as mass movements around the world seek civilizational alternatives to capitalist modernity.

Global South as an Epistemic Location

The emphasis on the Global South as an epistemic location needs to be contextualized because there is a deafening silence with respect to Southern thinkers in development thought. Social sciences and mainstream economics in particular have played a very big role in rendering invisible voices from the Global South, but this silence, it must be noted, is not confined to a particular field alone and is endemic to the structure of global knowledge production, which has tended to be North-centric and has downplayed concerns raised by Southern epistemologies (de Sousa Santos 2018). For quite some time now, radical critics of Eurocentrism have pointed out that the relative disdain with which non-Western thought has been treated is not so much a coincidence or a mere oversight but rather a reflection of the manner in which the global epistemological landscape has evolved over the past few centuries (Quijano 2007; Grosfoguel 2007). The rise of the West, as has been widely noted, went hand in hand with its domination of non-Western regions, but, and this is crucial, what is often missed is that this imperialist project was sustained and undergirded by an "epistemic strategy", which sought to "construct a hierarchy of superior and inferior knowledge and, thus, of superior and inferior people around the world" (Grosfoguel 2007: 214).

Postcolonial and decolonial critiques have successfully uncovered the complicity between Empire, racialized capitalism and knowledge production and have faulted the idea of endogenous European origins of modernity for discounting other historical accounts of modernity (Bhambra 2014: 117). Imbricated as they are in colonialism and coloniality, the afterlife of colonialism beyond its historical duration persists well into our own times. The coloniality of knowledge is the seductive power of European universality as "a way of participating . . . to reach the same material benefits and the same power as the Europeans: viz, to conquer nature, in short for 'development'" (Quijano 2007: 169). The corrective to such a claim of homogenous universality, therefore, urges for reconstructing historical narratives (Bhambra 2014: 117), remembering repressed and masked colonial histories, not in silos but as entangled, interlocking histories of the emergence of the modern world order (Manjapra 2020: 6–7), and reconfiguring what constitutes knowledge and what reads as theory, even if it is "not recognizable by the Eurocentric 'cosmopolitan' model" (Spivak 2018: xi).

This book takes decolonial critique as its starting point as it attempts to map the innovative engagements of thinkers from India and Latin America, with the aim of reflecting upon the development discourses these peripheral regions and former colonies have generated *vis-à-vis* their respective colonial/ postcolonial pathways. It highlights the manner in which thinkers from these two regions disrupted and challenged the hierarchies of global knowledge production.

The decolonial option, as the "singular connector of a diversity of de-colonials" who share in common "the colonial wound, the fact that regions and people around the world have been classified as underdeveloped econom-ically and mentally" (Mignolo 2009: 3), is a call for building alternatives to the coloniality of knowledge. To decolonize is not merely to emphasize "dif-ference", although this is how the decolonial option has come to be consumed by Western academia today. It is, as Frantz Fanon, Amílcar Cabral and many others have insisted, to seek to widen the limits of knowledge and broaden philosophies of liberation (Wood 2020; Colpani 2022). This requires employ-ing an interdisciplinary, global and comparative perspective in the humanities and social sciences to encompass disparate experiences of racialized coloniality (Manjapra 2020). As de Sousa Santos puts it, "the epistemologies of the South call for establishing bridges between comfort and discomfort zones, between the familiar and the strange fields of domination and of struggle" (de Sousa Santos 2018: 118). Reclaiming this interconnectedness is important because at the heart of Eurocentrism is a hermitic separatism, a blindness to how bridges and connections between societies have animated human exist-ence for centuries (Quijano 1993; Hobson 2004; Dussel 1997). It is this tradi-tion of intercultural dialogue that the decolonial option seeks to recover and, in the process, build "a renovated culture, which is not merely decolonized, but is moreover entirely new . . . is neither modern nor post-modern, but rather in a strict sense 'trans-modern'" (Dussel 2012: 50).

To be sure, the decolonial field consists of a spectrum of theoretical and political positions. Some, like Mignolo (2011), privilege "difference" and in-terpret the decolonial option as a project of de-modernization and epistemic delinking from Western thought. Others, like Quijano and Dussel, on the other hand, see in decolonization a project of inter-cultural dialogue aimed at widening liberatory horizons, a project that Fanon (2001: 253) interpreted as one that would enable "bringing the problem of mankind to an infinitely higher plane". With this understanding, this book takes the decolonial cri-tique as its starting point and highlights common intellectual themes that have emerged from thinkers in Latin America and India. The central argument of this book is that political, spatial and historical distinctions notwithstanding, the experiences of peripheralization, their common traditions of resistance to oppression and their deeply entangled histories have forged a shared intellec-tual identity that, while drawing on the most radical traditions of the Western enlightenment, has also sought to creatively transcend their limitations. And in the process, this shared intellectual project has built up a rich alternative set of emancipatory epistemologies grounded in the realities and histories of Southern nations.

Setting the Stage

The neoliberal transition in the developing world, which began in the 1980s, entailed a drastic rupture with post-War policymaking, but what is often missed is that it also involved a wholescale restructuring of the intellectual project that had undergirded the post-colonial era. For three decades prior to the neoliberal transition, countries across the Global South experimented with innovative policies aimed at breaking the economic and political stranglehold that advanced capitalist nations had exerted on them for over four centuries. The exact mix of strategies varied by region, but what tied them all together was a common sentiment of anti-imperialism and a recognition that "European history was transcended and unrepeatable" (Wolfe 1997: 394). It is worth emphasizing here that, contrary to neoliberal caricatures, these experiments were neither products of misplaced intellectual fads nor were they simply impositions from above by nationalist politicians seeking popularity with their base (Panagariya 2008; Edwards 2010, 2019).[2] Quite to the contrary, these experiments and the intellectual justifications they engendered were products of mass struggles, and thus the most crucial features that we identify with the post-War project in the Global South actually grew out of the demands raised by anti-colonial, anti-feudal movements that had sprung up across Asia, Africa and Latin America in the early half of the 20th century.[3] Through their struggles and experiences, these insurgent voices came to believe that the economic marginalization of the Third World was not, as the colonizers had asserted, a result of the cultural or racial inferiority of non-European peoples but instead a result of the violent colonial relations between the Euro-Atlantic and the non-European world, which had drained the latter of its resources and turned it into a large agrarian backyard for their industries (Naoroji 1996; Fanon 2001). As Fanon forcefully put it, "Europe is literally a creation of the Third World" (Fanon 2001: 83).

This hidden colonial base of European development, however, also meant that the entire idea of catching up or imitating the Western path to development was misplaced. Such a view missed the fact that

> when the West had been undergoing its own momentous development, there had not been another 'West' already there. Rather, there had been colonies, whose exploitation had historically produced – and, in changing ways, continued to produce – the paramountcy of the West. In other words, the great global fact that modernization theory obscured in representing Western history as autochthonous and repeatable was that development and underdevelopment were not two distinct states but a relationship.
>
> (Wolfe 1997: 395)

Europe was therefore doubly "indefensible" (Césaire 2000: 32): it was not only indefensible morally for all the brutality it had unleashed on non-European peoples but also indefensible as a model worthy of emulation for the Third World going forward. Freedom from colonial rule had to aspire to move beyond "English rule without the Englishman" (Gandhi 2009); it had to recognize the historical specificity of the challenges that underdeveloped nations faced, and even as it gazed with admiration towards Euro-American thought and practices, this "ideal of transparent universality" had to be modified, enriched and if required, even confronted and transcended, for after all, as Édouard Glissant had suggested, "the West is not in the West: it is a project not a place" (1989: 2).

"The Third World" too, in that sense, "was not a place. It was a project" (Prashad 2007: xv). And it was precisely this project that neoliberalism sought to displace. To be sure, the post-War experiments, ambitious as they were, never really succeeded in putting into practice all that they professed, and the contradictions between rhetoric and practice ultimately pushed them towards a severe crisis. But while the crisis itself, which started to become evident in the 1970s, created opportunities for neoliberalism to emerge, its eventual rise was in no way fated as the Vietnamese and Nicaraguan revolutions clearly indicated. The fact that neoliberal forces were eventually successful in overturning post-War projects was that they were able to construct and diffuse a new "common sense", which held that there was no alternative to globalized capitalism and that the follies of post-War developmentalism arose not so much from the contradictions of capitalism but exactly the opposite – from the fact that these projects did not fully unchain capitalist forces (Chodor 2014). The coercive imposition of neoliberal adjustments on developing countries has been widely commented upon, but one must, in this context, not underestimate how important the ideological assault of neoliberal forces in universities, policy making institutions and privately funded think tanks turned out to be (Klein 2007). Economists spearheaded the assault. Within universities, rabidly conservative schools of economics became hegemonic even as Keynesian, institutionalist and radical streams came to be overshadowed (Blyth 2002). The American and European academy led the transformation, but these ideas soon found their way over to the developing world as well, as PhDs from American and European universities trained in orthodox mainstream economics filled up university spaces, central banks, planning commissions and other nodal agencies of policy making (Mudge 2008; Glassman 1999). This was aided by changes within the mainstream economics discipline itself, which increasingly emphasized the use of formal mathematical tools, thus imparting a scientific, universal aura to its theories that were in reality unabashedly pro-neoliberal. Moreover, this shift also aided a kind of "methodological universalism" that had always dogged neoclassical theory but which started to become even more pervasive in the post-1970 decades. The discipline came to emphasize

abstract, universal reasoning in terms of "representative agents" and "representative economy", with an essentially metaphorical connection to real-life situations . . . detached from their local (historical and geographical) context . . . generally understood to be instances of some universal phenomena.

(Fourcade 2006: 160)

Gone were the voices from the Third World that insisted on the historical specificity of underdeveloped nations and pointed to the distinctive nature of their developmental experiences. In its place was a discourse that emphasized homogeneity and insisted on using the West's experiences as universal templates that merely needed to be grafted onto non-Western economies (Mehmet 2002).

Today, as we stand on the rubble of economic devastation caused by neoliberal policies, these words are a reminder of just how misplaced the fanfare and optimism with which neoliberalism was greeted by several influential voices were. There is little doubt today that we are in the midst of what Foster (2013) refers to as an "epochal crisis" marked by a closing in, or rather a binding of, ecological, economic and social constraints on capitalist accumulation. The threat of climate change and all the environmental consequences that it entails, combined with growing financialization and the deepening dependence of capitalism on low wage labour, mark a new, and in a Leninist sense, literally "final" stage of capitalism. Finality here, of course, does not derive from some mechanical inevitability of collapse but rather from the simple fact that the destructive tendencies that this system has come to rely upon have now gone to such an extent that our very planetary existence is at stake.

The wealth of development ideas that have emanated from India and Latin America has been the subject of several scholarly works (Klein 1973; Chandra 1991; Dasgupta 2002; Zachariah 2005; Kay 2010; Caldentey and Vernengo 2007; Garcia-Molina and Trautwein 2016; Valencia 2017; Trincado *et al.* 2020; Sridevi 2020; Bach 2018). This book not only builds on these studies but also seeks to extend them by placing the intellectual efforts of thinkers from the two regions in a comparative and relational perspective. Doing so is necessary for two reasons. First, existing studies mentioned earlier have largely taken nation states as their units of analysis, which, while valuable in its own right, tends to miss how the interlocking experiences of marginalization, poverty and imperialism in the peripheries of the modern world system have produced parallel strands of thinking in otherwise unconnected geographical locales. Recognizing how "processes or tendencies that developed on a global scale or to use comparison to elaborate on the different processes or tendencies that developed in different parts of the world or in different eras" is necessary to expand academic lenses beyond the West and to make development thought more diverse (Moyn and Sartori 2013: 7). Second, beyond uncovering striking parallels, a global analysis is also important because ideas rarely respect the political and cultural boundaries that academicians tend to take as their starting points. Historians of intellectual thought have of late begun to emphasize how global connectedness and historical entanglements are crucial to understanding the evolution of ideas (Moyn and Sartori 2013; Manjapra 2020; Armitage 2004). Intellectuals from the Global South during the short 20th century, which is roughly the period that this book focuses on, straddled multiple worlds, travelled extensively and sought out alternative paths between "the colourless vagueness of cosmopolitanism" and "the fierce self-idolatry of nation-worship" (Rabindranath Tagore cited in Williams 2007: 71). The catastrophic world wars in the West, interspersed with the Russian Revolution and mass anti-colonial movements in the East, weakened imperial claims over civilizational ideals. The search for new imaginaries and alternative models of social life drove intellectuals to seek refuge beyond the borders of the empire. Tagore's travels to Latin America "inspired a generation of young intellectuals keen to rethink their country's relationship with Europe" (Goebel 2015: 260) and for Mariátegui, the "Chinese model had enough similarity and notably enough difference to afford . . . a distinctively concrete, fecund, and evolving example by which to formulate a new Peruvian praxis" (Kim 2015: 173). These horizontal dialogues had echoes throughout the second half of the 20th century in the "transnational anti-imperialist solidarities" reflected in Bandung and the Tricontinental (Mahler 2018: 24).

The hidden, entangled histories of South-South interactions have started to attract attention, but studies on intellectual and cultural interrelationships between India and Latin America in a comparative framework are only beginning to emerge. Examples of such studies would be Susanne Klengel and Alexandra Ortiz Wallner's edited book *Sur/South: Poetics and Politics of Thinking Latin America/India* (2016), which brings together essays of Latin Americanists from the United States, Europe, Latin America and India working on India-Latin America cultural and intellectual encounters. Stephanie Rivera Berruz and Leah Kalmanson's *Comparative Studies in Asian and Latin American Philosophies: Cross-Cultural Theories and Methodologies* (2018) focuses on comparative philosophy. This collection of essays, as the title shows, is focused on Asia and Latin America and not specifically on India, and its subject matter and methodology are comparative philosophy. Roanne L. Kantor's study, *South Asian Writers, Latin American Literature, and the Rise of Global English* (2022), is an important recent contribution aimed at studying the interconnections between Latin American and South Asian writing from the 1960s and 1970s in the context of Global Anglophone literature. Studies on India-Latin America relations from an international relations, innovation policy, foreign policy, trade and political dialogue perspective are available (Bhojwani 2015; Gonzalo 2022; Nafey *et al.* 2012; Uchmany 1998), as are books focusing specifically on Brazil and India, particularly after BRICS (Loundo and Misse 2003; Sirohi 2019). There have been a number of studies on the literary encounter between India and Latin America, particularly on Rabindranath Tagore's encounter with writers and intellectuals in Argentina, beginning with the pioneering study of Ketaki Kushari Dyson (1988). Recently there have been several focused studies on Latin America's engagement with Asia (López-Calvo 2007, 2010, 2012; Gasquet 2020; Gasquet and Majstorovic 2021; Lu and Camps 2020). However, a simple count of the essays in these volumes will reveal that they focus mainly on Latin America's engagement with Japan and China, or the Arab world.

There is a need for monographic works on Indian/Latin American epistemic engagement, a gap this book aims to fill.

Plan of the Book

With this theoretical and methodological framework elaborated upon in this introduction, the rest of the book is divided into three chapters built around three salient themes.

Chapter 1 draws on the writings of Dadabhai Naoroji (1825–1917) from India and Raúl Prebisch (1901–1986) from Argentina and highlights the original manner in which thinkers from these two outposts visualized the interconnections between economic development and the dynamics of global imperium. Much of the recent literature in mainstream development economics that analyses differential patterns of development has tended to miss the global, multi-scalar and relational nature of the process (Acemoglu *et al.* 2001, 2002; Sachs 2003; Engerman and Sokoloff 2005; Spolaore and Wacziarg 2009). By viewing development in this narrow manner, these theories have ended up downplaying international connections between regions that have been so crucial to shaping our global economic landscape (Sirohi 2017; Ince 2022). Surprisingly, this lacuna dogs several heterodox streams of thinking as well (Warren 1980; Harvey 2003, 2007).[4] As a result, much of the existing literature, both orthodox and heterodox, tirelessly repeats old Eurocentric arguments and completely misses the complex web of global interlinkages between the Western and the non-Western worlds that have been so crucial in reproducing global development disparities till this very day (Patnaik and Patnaik 2021). By contrast, we argue that a striking theme that keeps reappearing in the writings of several 20th-century thinkers from India and Latin America is precisely the centrality of global imperialist dynamics in shaping and directing development in the peripheral world (Naoroji 1996; Dutt 2103a, 2103b; Mariátegui 2011; Prebisch 1950; Prebisch 1980; Marini 1972; Nehru 2008; Gandhi 2009). Voices from these two outposts repeatedly hammered home their contention that the poverty of their respective regions could never truly be comprehended unless it was placed in an international context and, more importantly, in the context of the imperialist dominance of European powers. The centrality of imperialist dynamics was, of course, something that was commented upon by European thinkers as well (Hilferding 1910; Bukharin 2010; Lenin 1974; Luxemburg 2003). In fact, traditionally, when one speaks of imperialism, the term itself is often associated with stalwarts of the European socialist movement who used it as an umbrella term to describe European militarism during the interwar years. But the striking fact is that even as these European debates produced a rich corpus of innovative thinking on capital's global expansionism, the parameters of the debate remained geographically confined and thus revolved around a European perspective with little emphasis being placed on the role of the peripheries (Brewer 1990; Callinicos 2009).[5]

In contrast, we shall show that not only was imperialism a central category of analysis in Southern thought, but that the manner in which it was theorized was novel because it emphasized the centrality of the role played by non-Western regions, thus decentring Europe as the pivot of the world economy. Whereas classical theories of imperialism (Marxist as well as non-Marxist ones) predicted massive exports of capital from the North to the South as a core feature of capitalism in its imperialist "phase", and predicted that such outflows of wealth would lead to a universalization of the capitalist mode of production across the world, the *differentia specifica* of Southern thought was its emphasis on the reverse flow of resources from the South to the North and the belief that integration with the global economy would thwart rather than promote development even along capitalist lines (Naoroji 1996; Dutt 2013a, 2013b; Marini 1972; Furtado 2021). Moreover, while the emphasis of their writings was understandably on the negative effects of international linkages, many Southern thinkers viewed the relationship between the local and global economic forces dialectically and thus emphasized the multi-scalar nature of underdevelopment, giving due weight to structural dimensions of underdevelopment as well (Ranade 2014; Furtado 2016; Sunkel 1969; Prebisch 1980, 1985; Prebisch 1950).

Chapter 2 will revisit the issue of social identities. A salient feature of many writings that came out of Latin America and India was the recognition of the fact that their experiences were distinct from those of the West and that even as colonialism pinned onto their societies new laws, institutions and relations of production, the process always remained partial, resulting in a complex interweaving of different forms of time (Mercado 2017; Furtado 2021; Gandhi 2009). Thus, even as Southern nations became inextricably drawn into the vortex of global capitalism, their incorporation produced a mix of temporalities in which older forms of social organization existed side by side and in constant interaction with newer forms. This peculiar compression meant that, unlike in the West, where relations of production come to be seen as being mediated by economic forces alone, in the Global South, the pattern of accumulation comes to be seen as relying on a complex admixture of economic and non-economic forces. This meant that whereas classical political economists like Smith and Ricardo, or even far more sensitive thinkers like Marx, never really focused their attention on the salience of non-economic identities, writers from the Global South placed the issues of caste, race and ethnic identities right at the centre of their thinking and commented extensively on the complex interweaving of imperialism, class relations and identity in their respective regions (Mercado 2017; Phule 2002; Ambedkar 2014, 2016; Mariátegui 1971; Casanova 1965; Cotler 1967; Quijano 2000). This chapter draws on the writings of José Carlos Mariátegui (1894–1930) and B.R. Ambedkar (1891–1956), who were contemporaries and who wrote extensively on issues of race and caste, respectively. Their emphasis on the structural underpinnings of racism and casteism challenges both the orthodox Marxist stance – which has hitherto relegated non-economic identities to the margins of revolutionary theory because of their purported insignificance in determining the motions of capitalist development (Wood 2000; Harvey 2014; Karat 2011) – as well as the classical liberal view that reduces social oppression to a matter of individual tastes and preferences (Becker 1971; Arrow 1998). The recent upsurge in social movements across the world foregrounding issues of race, caste, gender and ethnicity, as well as the recognition of the racial nature of capitalism, have brought social identities to the forefront of political and academic discussions, and it is here that the writings of Mariátegui and Ambedkar can provide a useful entry point.

The final theme that this book looks at in Chapter 3 is the circulation of ideas between India and Latin America and the non-hierarchical horizontal dialogue amongst the peripheral intellectuals of the two regions. While their encounter with Europe happened under imperial eyes, their approximation to each other's intellectual thought has been vital to their epistemic self-constitution and to the imaginary of the Global South. Given the different historical trajectory of Latin America's anti-colonial project, its connections with the Afro-Asian projects of political and economic sovereignty, which gave rise to transnational anti-imperialist networks, and wherein lie the origins of the idea of the Global South, are only beginning to be studied in their entirety. These entanglements serve as concrete examples of decolonial experimentation and thus have to be uncovered, recovered and their trajectory reconstructed in order to potentiate the argument that these regions are producers of ideas. The 1967 Nobel Laureate for literature, Miguel Ángel Asturias (Guatemala, 1899–1974), accompanied by his wife Blanca Mora y Araujo, came to India to attend the Asian Writers' Conference held in December 1956 in New Delhi. Subsequently, Asturias published several chronicles on his sojourn in India, which appeared in the column he used to write in *El Nacional*, the Venezuelan daily from Caracas. These chronicles of India and Asia in general cover several themes ranging from language, culture and history to the contemporary dilemmas of writers and intellectuals. Asturias and Blanca Araujo also translated Indian writer Bhabani Bhattacharya's 1954 novel *He Who Rides a Tiger* into Spanish. These texts and Asturias's engagement with India remain a surprisingly under-examined aspect of the Nobel Laureate's oeuvre. The chapter focuses on this visit and the texts that Asturias wrote after it in order to reconstruct the post-Bandung cultural consolidation of the imaginary of the Third World beyond Asia and Africa by including Latin America in this transnational flow of ideas. We argue that these chronicles embody "the Bandung spirit" and constitute an important body of texts that pre-figure the synergy of intellectual thought in the framework of South-South exchange that would be seen subsequently in the intellectual encounters between India and Latin America.

The chapters that follow attempt to weave together the intellectual threads that have emerged from India and Latin America. They challenge the old

Eurocentric division of the world into a permanent, theory-producing core and a permanent, theory-absorbing periphery by asserting the Global South as an epistemic location. The chapters show how parallel experiences of marginalization have produced a corpus of ideas, categories and frameworks that, far from being localized and insular in their reach, have a certain translatability and generalizability beyond their local confines. Thus, as it looks back at key moments of the 19th and 20th centuries through the relational prism of development thought, this volume seeks to subvert the established assumptions of what constitutes knowledge and challenge epistemic injustices that continue to shape the global knowledge landscape.

Notes

1 For the traditional neoliberal critiques of developmentalism, see Krueger (1998) and Bhagwati (1993). Panagariya (2011) provides an updated statement of the neoliberal critique in the aftermath of the 2008 Global Financial Crisis.
2 The notion of development has been heavily criticized by post-colonial scholarship as well. Development, post-colonial scholarship asserts, provided justifications for colonial rule and an ideological cover for the continued oppression of subaltern classes by nationalist elites in the Global South in the post-colonial era (Chakrabarty 2008; Mehta 1999).
3 For an account of these anti-imperialist developmentalisms, see Temin (2023) and Marwah 2019)
4 There have been several notable exceptions. Recent years have seen an intellectual effervescence on issues of dependency, unequal exchange and imperialism (Sirohi 2017; Sirohi and Bhupatiraju 2021; Kvangraven 2021; Antunes de Oliveira 2022; Suwandi 2019). But overall, these discussions have remained marginal compared to discussions within heterodox economics circles.
5 Lenin's writings were exceptions to this trend. While Lenin's post-1914 writings on imperialism are well known, it is worth noting that he closely followed anti-colonial movements in countries like India well before the outbreak of the First World War. From 1914 on, anti-colonial struggles became even more central to his political and intellectual project. As Anderson (2007: 128) states, he "was the first major political theorist, Marxist or non-Marxist, to grasp the importance that anti-imperialist national movements would have for global politics in the twentieth century".

References

Acemoglu, D., Johnson, S. and Robinson, J. A. (2001). The Colonial Origins of Comparative Development: An Empirical Investigation. *American Economic Review*, 91 (5), 1369–1401.

Acemoglu, D., Johnson, S. and Robinson, J. A. (2002). Reversal of Fortune: Geography and Institutions in the Making of the Modern World Income Distribution. *Quarterly Journal of Economics*, 107 (4), 1231–1294.

Ambedkar, B. R. (2014). The Untouchables and the Pax Britannica. In *Dr. Babasaheb Ambedkar, Writings and Speeches*, Vol. 12. New Delhi: Dr. Ambedkar Foundation, Ministry of Social Justice and Empowerment, Govt. of India.

Ambedkar, B. R. (2016). *Annihilation of Caste: The Annotated Critical Edition*. New Delhi: Navayana Publishing.

Anderson, K. B. (2007). The Rediscovery and Persistence of the Dialectic in Philosophy and in World Politics. In S. Budgen, S. Kouvelakis, and S. Žižek (Eds.), *Lenin Reloaded: Towards a Politics of Truth*. Durham and London: Duke University Press, 120–147.

Antunes de Oliveira, F. (2022). Lost and Found: Bourgeois Dependency Theory and the Forgotten Roots of Neodevelopmentalism. *Latin American Perspectives*, 49 (1), 36–56.

Armitage, D. (2004). 'The Fifty Years' Rift: Intellectual History and International Relations, *Modern Intellectual History*, 1 (1), 97–109.

Arrow, K. J. (1998). What Has Economics to Say About Racial Discrimination? *Journal of Economic Perspectives*, 12 (2), 91–100.

Bach, M. (2018). What Laws Determine Progress? An Indian Contribution to the Idea of Progress Based on Mahadev Govind Ranade's Works, 1870–1901. *The European Journal of the History of Economic Thought*, 25 (2), 327–356.

Becker, G. S. (1971). *The Economics of Discrimination*. Chicago: University of Chicago Press.

Berruz, S. R. and Kalmanson L. (2018). *Comparative Studies in Asian and Latin American Philosophies: Cross-Cultural Theories and Methodologies*. London: Bloomsbury.

Bhagwati, J. (1993). *India in Transition: Freeing the Economy*. Oxford: Clarendon Press.

Bhambra, G. K. (2014). Postcolonial and Decolonial Reconstructions. In *Connected Sociologies*. London: Bloomsbury Academic, 117–140.

Bhojwani, D. (2012). *Latin America, the Caribbean and India: Promise and Challenge*. New Delhi: Pentagon Press/ICWA.

Blyth, M. (2002). *Great Transformations: Economic Ideas and Institutional Change in the Twentieth Century*. Cambridge, UK: Cambridge University Press.

Brewer, T. (1990). *Marxist Theories of Imperialism: A Critical Survey*. 2nd edition. London: Routledge.

Bukharin, N. (2010). *Imperialism and World Economy*. New Delhi: Aakar Books.

Caldentey, E. P. and Vernengo, M. (Eds.) (2007). *Ideas, Policies and Economic Development in the Americas*. New York: Routledge.

Callinicos, A. (2009). *Imperialism and Global Political Economy*. Cambridge: Polity Press.

Casanova, P. G. (1965). Internal Colonialism and National Development. *Studies in Comparative International Development*, 1 (4), 27–37.

Césaire, A. (2000). *Discourse on Colonialism*. New York: Monthly Review Press.

Chakrabarty, D. (2008). *Provincializing Europe: Postcolonial Thought and Historical Difference*. Princeton, NJ: Princeton University Press.

Chandra, B. (1991). Colonial India: British Versus Indian Views of Development. *Review (Fernand Braudel Center)*, 14 (1), 81–167.

Chodor, T. (2014). *Neoliberal Hegemony and the Pink Tide in Latin America: Breaking Up With TINA?* Hoboken, NJ: Palgrave Macmillan.

Colpani, G. (2022). Crossfire: Postcolonial Theory between Marxist and Decolonial Critiques. *Postcolonial Studies*, 25 (1), 54–72.

Cotler, J. (1967). The Mechanisms of Internal Domination and Social Change in Peru. *Studies in Comparative International Development*, 3 (12), 229–246.

Dasgupta, A. K. (2002). *A History of Indian Economic Thought*. London: Routledge.

de Sousa Santos, B. (2018). *The End of the Cognitive Empire: The Coming of Age of Epistemologies of the South*. Durham, NC: Duke University Press.

Dussel, E. D. (1997). *The Invention of the Americas: Eclipse of "the Other" and the Myth of Modernity*. New York: Continuum Press.

Dussel, E. D. (2012). Transmodernity and Interculturality: An Interpretation From the Perspective of Philosophy of Liberation. *Transmodernity: Journal of Peripheral Cultural Production of the Luso-Hispanic World*, 1 (3), 28–59.

Dutt, R. C. (2013a). *The Economic History of India Under Early British Rule: From the Rise of the British power in 1757 to the Accession of Queen Victoria in 1837*. London: Routledge.

Dutt, R. C. (2013b). *The Economic of History of India in the Victorian Age: From the Accession of Queen Victoria in 1837 to the Commencement of the Twentieth Century*, London: Routledge.

Dyson, K. K. (1988): *In Your Blossoming Flower-Garden: Rabindranath Tagore and Victoria Ocampo*. New Delhi: Sahitya Akademi.

Edwards, S. (2010). *Left Behind: Latin America and the False Promise of Populism*. Chicago: University of Chicago Press.

Edwards, S. (2019). On Latin American Populism, and Its Echoes around the World. *Journal of Economic Perspectives*, 33 (4), 76–99.

Engerman, S. L. and Sokoloff , K. L. (2005). *Colonialism, Inequality, and Long-run Paths of Development*, NBER Working Paper No. 11057, Cambridge, Mass.: National Bureau of Economic Research.

Fanon, F. (2001). *The Wretched of the Earth*. London: Penguin Books.

Filippini, F. and Yeyati, E. L. (2022). *Pandemic Divergence: A Short Note on Covid-19 and Global Income Inequality*, Brookings Working Paper No. 168, London: Brookings Institution.

Foster, J. B. (2013). The Epochal Crisis. *Monthly Review*, 65 (5), 1–12.

Fourcade, M. (2006). The Construction of a Global Profession: The Transnationalization of Economics. *American Journal of Sociology*, 112 (1), 145–194.

Furtado, C. (2016). Development and Underdevelopment. In R. Bielschowsky (Ed.), *ECLAC Thinking: Selected Texts, 1948–1998*. Santiago De Chile: ECLAC, 141–148.

Furtado, C. (2021). The Myth of Economic Development and the Future of the Third World. *Review of Political Economy*, 33 (1), 16–27.

Gandhi, M. K. (2009). Hind Swaraj. In A. Parel (Ed.), *M. K. Gandhi: Hind Swaraj and Other Writings*. Cambridge University Press.

Garcia-Molina, M. and Trautwein, H. M. (Eds.) (2016). *Peripheral Visions of Economic Development: New Frontiers in Development Economics and the History of Economic Thought*. London: Routledge.

Gasquet, A. (2020). *Argentine Literary Orientalism: From Esteban Echeverria to Roberto Arlt*. Hoboken, NJ: Palgrave Macmillan.

Gasquet, A. and Majstorovic G. (Eds.) (2021). *Cultural and Literary Dialogues Between Asia and Latin America*. London: Palgrave Macmillan.

Gereffi, G. (2020). What Does the COVID-19 Pandemic Teach us about Global Value Chains? The Case of Medical Supplies. *Journal of International Business Policy*, 3, 287–301.

Glassman, J. (1999). State Power beyond the Territorial Trap: The Internationalization of the State. *Political Geography,* 18 (6), 669–696.

Glissant, É. (1989). *Caribbean Discourse: Selected Essays.* Translated by J. Michael Dash. Charlottesville: University Press of Virginia.

Goebel, M. (2015). Vernacularizing Nationalism: An Outcome Foretold? In *Anti-Imperial Metropolis: Interwar Paris and the Seeds of Third World Nationalism* (Global and International History). Cambridge: Cambridge University Press, 250–278.

Gonzalo, M. (2022). *India from Latin America: Peripherisation, Statebuilding, and Demand-Led Growth.* New York: Routledge.

Ghosh, J. (2020). A Critique of the Indian Government's Response to the COVID-19 Pandemic. *Journal of Industrial and Business Economics,* 47 (3), 519–530.

Gramsci, A. (1971). *Selections From the Prison Notebooks.* New York: International Publishers.

Grosfoguel, R. (2007). The Epistemic Decolonial Turn: Beyond Political-Economy Paradigms. *Cultural Studies,* 21 (2–3), 211–223.

Harvey, D. (2003). *The New Imperialism.* Oxford: Oxford University Press.

Harvey, D. (2007). *A Brief History of Neoliberalism.* New York: Oxford University Press.

Harvey, D. (2014). *Seventeen Contradictions and the End of Capitalism.* New York: Oxford University Press.

Hilferding, R (1910). *Finance Capital: A Study of the Latest Phase of Capitalist Development.* Retrieved from: www.marxists.org/archive/hilferding/1910/finkap/index. htm [Viewed 22/03/2023]

Hobson, J. M. (2004). *The Eastern Origins of Western Civilisation.* Cambridge: Cambridge University Press.

Ince, O. U. (2022). Saving Capitalism From Empire: Uses of Colonial History in New Institutional Economics. *International Relations,* 0(0). https://doi.org/10.1177/00471178221104699.

Jomo, K. S., and Chowdhury, A. (2020). COVID-19 Pandemic Recession and Recovery. *Development,* 63 (2), 226–237.

Kantor, R. L. (2022). *South Asian Writers, Latin American Literature and the Rise of Global English.* New York: Cambridge University Press.

Karat, P. (2011). The Challenge of Identity Politics. *The Marxist,* 27 (1–2), 39–50.

Kay, C. (2010). *Latin American Theories of Development and Under Development.* London: Routledge.

Kesar, S., Abraham, R., Lahoti, R., Nath, P., & Basole, A. (2021). Pandemic, informality, and vulnerability: Impact of COVID-19 on livelihoods in India. *Canadian Journal of Development Studies,* 42 (1–2), 145–164.

Kim, D. H. (2015). José Mariátegui's East-South Decolonial Experiment. *Comparative and Continental Philosophy,* 7 (2), 157–179.

Klein, I. (1973). Indian Nationalism and Anti-industrialization: The Roots of Gandhian Economics. *South Asia: Journal of South Asian Studies,* 3 (1), 93–104.

Klein, N. (2007). *The Shock Doctrine: The Rise of Disaster Capitalism.* New York: Metropolitan Books.

Klengel, S. and Ortiz Wallner, A. (2016). *Sur/South: Poetics and Politics of Thinking Latin America/India.* Berlin: Iberoamericana-Vervuert.

Krueger, A. O. (1998). Why Trade Liberalisation Is Good for Growth. *Economic Journal,* 108, 1513–1522.

16 Introduction

Kvangraven, I. H. (2021). Beyond the Stereotype: Restating the Relevance of the Dependency Research Programme. *Development and Change*, 52 (1), 76–112.

Lenin, V. I. (1974). Imperialism, the Highest Stage of Capitalism, *Lenin Collected Works Vol 22* Moscow: Progress Publishers.

Liebman, A., Rhiney, K., and Wallace, R. (2020). To Die a Thousand Deaths: COVID-19, Racial Capitalism, and Anti-Black Violence. *Human Geography*, 13 (3), 331–335.

López-Calvo, I. (2007). *Alternative Orientalisms in Latin America and Beyond*. Newcastle: Cambridge Scholars Publishing.

López-Calvo, I. (2010). *One World Periphery Reads the Other: Knowing the "Oriental" in the Americas and the Iberian Peninsula*. Newcastle: Cambridge Scholars Publishing.

López-Calvo, I. (Ed.) (2012). *Peripheral Transmodernities South-to-South Intercultural Dialogues Between the Luso-Hispanic World and "the Orient"*. Newcastle: Cambridge Scholars Publishing.

Loundo, D. and Misse, M. (Eds.) (2003). *Diálogos Tropicais: Brasil e Índia*. Rio de Janeiro: Editora da UFRJ.

Lu, J. and Camps, M. (Eds.) (2020). *Transpacific Literary and Cultural Connections: Latin American Influence in India*. Palgrave Macmillan.

Luxemburg, R. (2003). *The Accumulation of Capital*. London and New York, NY: Routledge.

Mahler, A. G. (2018). *From the Tricontinental to the Global South: Race, Radicalism, and Transnational Solidarity*. Durham, NC: Duke University Press.

Manjapra, K. (2020). *Colonialism in Global Perspective*. Cambridge: Cambridge University Press.

Mariátegui, J. C. (1971). *Seven Interpretative Essays on Peruvian Reality*. Austin: University of Texas Press. Retrieved from: www.marxists.org/archive/mariateg/works/7-interpretive-essays/index.htm [Viewed 11/07/2020]

Mariátegui, J. C. (2011). Colonial Economy. In H. E. Vanden and M. Becker (Eds.), *José Carlos Mariátegui: An Anthology*. New York: Monthly Review Press, 122–123.

Marini, R. M. (1972). La Acumulación Capitalista Dependiente y la Superexplotación del Trabajo. Retrieved from: https://marini-escritos.unam.mx/?p=1221 [Viewed 22/03/2023]

Marwah, I. S. (2019). Provincializing Progress: Developmentalism and Anti-imperialism in Colonial India. *Polity*, 51 (3), 498–531.

Marx, K. (1887). *Capital*, Vol. 1. Moscow: Progress Publishers. Retrieved from: www.marxists.org

Mehmet, O. (2002). *Westernizing the Third World: The Eurocentricity of Economic Development Theories*. London: Routledge.

Mehta, U. S. (1999). *Liberalism and Empire: A Study in Nineteenth-Century British Liberal Thought*. Chicago, IL: University of Chicago Press.

Mercado, R. Z. (2017). *Towards a History of the National-Popular in Bolivia, 1879–1980*. Translated by A. Freeland. London, New York and Calcutta: Seagull Books.

Mignolo, W. D. (2009). Epistemic Disobedience, Independent Thought and De-Colonial Freedom, *Theory, Culture & Society*, 26 (7–8), 1–23.

Mignolo, W. D. (2011). Geopolitics of Sensing and Knowing: On (de) Coloniality, Border Thinking and Epistemic Disobedience. *Postcolonial studies*, 14 (3), 273–283.

Montes V. (2020). The Containment of COVID-19 Is Antithetical to the System of US Capitalism. *Human Geography*, 13 (3), 326–330.

Moyn, S. and Sartori, A. (2013). Approaches to Global Intellectual History. In S. Moyn and A. Sartori (Eds.), *Global Intellectual History*. New York: Columbia University Press, 3–30.

Mudge, S. L. (2008). The State of the Art: What Is Neo-liberalism? *Socio-Economic Review*, 6 (4), 703–731.

Nafey, A., Guzmán, E. and Feldmann, A. E. (Eds.) (2012). *Chile in the Age of Globalisation: Dialogue With India*. New Delhi: Manak Publications.

Naoroji, D. (1996). *Poverty and Un-British Rule in India*. 2nd edition. New Delhi: Publications Division, Ministry of Information and Broadcasting, Government of India.

Nehru, J. (2008). *Discovery of India*. London: Penguin.

Nelson A. (2020). COVID-19: Capitalist and Postcapitalist Perspectives. *Human Geography*, 13 (3), 305–309.

Panagariya, A. (2008). *India: The Emerging Giant*. Oxford: Oxford University Press.

Panagariya, A. (2011). A Re-examination of the Infant Industry Argument for Protection. *Margin: The Journal of Applied Economic Research*, 5 (1), 7–30.

Patnaik, U. and Patnaik, P. (2021). *Capital and Imperialism: Theory, History, and the Present*. New York: Monthly Review Press.

Phule, J (2002). Slavery. In G. R. Deshpande (Ed.), *Selected Writings of Jotirao Phule*. New Delhi: LeftWord Books, 23–100.

Panagariya, A. (2011). A Re-examination of the Infant Industry Argument for Protection. *Margin: The Journal of Applied Economic Research*, 5 (1), 7–30.

Prashad, V. (2007). *The Darker Nations: A People's History of the Third World*. New York and London: The New Press.

Prebisch, R. (1950). *The Economic Development of Latin America and Its Principal Problems*. New York: United Nations.

Prebisch, R. (1980). Towards a Theory of Change. *CEPAL Review*, 10, 155–208.

Prebisch, R. (1985). The Latin American Periphery in the Global Crisis of Capitalism. *CEPAL Review*, 26, 63–88.

Prebisch, R. (1950). *The Economic Development of Latin America and Its Principal Problems*. New York: United Nations.

Quijano, A. (1993). Modernity, Identity, and Utopia in Latin America. *Boundary 2*, 20 (3), 140–155.

Quijano, A. (2000). Coloniality of Power and Eurocentrism in Latin America. *International Sociology*, 15 (2), 215–232.

Quijano, A. (2007). Coloniality and Modernity/Rationality. *Cultural Studies*, 21 (2), 168–178.

Ranade, M. G. (2014). Indian Political Economy. In B. Chandra (Ed.), *Ranade's Economic Writings*. New Delhi: Gyan Publishing House, 322–349.

Sachs, J. D. (2003). *Institutions Don't Rule: Direct Effects of Geography on Per Capita Income*, NBER Working Paper No. 9490, Cambridge, MA: National Bureau of Economic Research.

Sirohi, R. A. (2017). Colonial 'Shock' and Global Inequalities: A Critical Review of New Institutional Economics. *Economic & Political Weekly*, 52 (33), 85–93.

Sirohi, R. A. (2019). *From Developmentalism to Neoliberalism: A Comparative Analysis of Brazil and India*. Singapore: Palgrave Macmillan.

Sirohi, R. A. and Bhupatiraju, S. (2021). *Reassessing the Pink Tide: Lessons From Brazil and Venezuela*. Singapore: Palgrave Macmillan.

Spivak, G. (2018). General Introduction. In René Zavaleta Mercado, *Towards a History of the National-Popular in Bolivia, 1879–1980*. Translated by A. Freeland. London, New York, Calcutta: Seagull Books, vi–xv.

Spolaore, E. and Wacziarg, R. (2009). The Diffusion of Development. *The Quarterly Journal of Economics*, 124 (2), 469–529.

Sridevi, G. (2020). *Ambedkar's Vision of Economic Development for India*. New Delhi: Routledge.

Sunkel, O. (1969). National Development Policy and External Dependence in Latin America. *The Journal of Development Studies*, 6 (1), 23–48.

Suwandi, I. (2019). *Value Chains: The New Economic Imperialism*. New York, NY: Monthly Review Press.

Temin, D. M. (2023). Development in Decolonization: Walter Rodney, Third World Developmentalism, and "Decolonizing Political Theory". *American Political Science Review*, 117 (1), 235–248.

Trincado, E., Lazzarini, A. and Melnik, D. (Eds.) (2020). *Ideas in the History of Economic Development: The Case of Peripheral Countries*. Routledge.

Uchmany, E. A. (Ed.) (1998). *México-India: Similitudes y encuentros a través de la historia*. México D.F.: FCE.

Valencia, A. S. (2017). *Sub-Imperialism Revisited: Dependency Theory in the Thought of Ruy Mauro Marini*. Leiden: Brill.

Warren, B. (1980). *Imperialism: Pioneer of Capitalism*. London: New Left Books.

Williams, L. B. (2007). Overcoming the "Contagion of Mimicry": The Cosmopolitan Nationalism and Modernist History of Rabindranath Tagore and WB Yeats. *The American Historical Review*, 112 (1), 69–100.

Wolfe, P. (1997). History and Imperialism: A Century of Theory, From Marx to Postcolonialism. *The American Historical Review*, 102 (2), 388–420.

Wood, D. A. (2020). *Epistemic Decolonization: A Critical Investigation Into the Anticolonial Politics of Knowledge*. Cham: Palgrave Macmillan.

Wood, E. M. (2000). *Democracy Against Capitalism: Renewing Historical Materialism*. Cambridge: Cambridge University Press.

Zachariah, B. (2005). *Developing India: An Intellectual and Social History c. 1930–50*. New Delhi: Oxford University Press.

1   Decolonizing Development

From Dadabhai Naoroji to Raúl Prebisch

It is often suggested that two rival traditions have existed side by side in economic thought since the 19th century: the "production-centred" approach, which not only dates back to classical political economists but also includes figures like Marx, and the "exchange-centred" approach, whose origins are usually traced back to the late 19th-century writings of Mill, Menger and Jevons (Garegnani 1984; Bharadwaj 1986; Lee and Jo 2011; Chang and Andreoni 2021). Whereas the former takes as its starting point social classes and centres its analysis on how conflict between these classes shapes the size, distribution and use of social surplus, the latter has primarily focused its efforts on studying markets and the competitive forces that shape their functioning. The differences accorded to the spheres of production and circulation in the two schools are crucial because these in turn have had enormous consequences for how each camp explains the dynamics of accumulation and distribution in capitalist formations. More precisely, whereas the production-centred approach, because of its emphasis on class conflict rooted in production structures, has tended to view capitalist formations as inherently unstable and crisis-prone, the exchange-centred approach has conceptualized capitalism as a rational and eternally stable system, autonomous in every sense from its social environment.

The twofold division between production and exchange-centred approaches has been extremely influential in heterodox circles because it has served as a potent corrective to the hegemonic claims of neoclassical orthodoxy and because it has served to clarify the shared grounds upon which heterodox approaches can be built (Lee and Jo 2011). But even as these taxonomies have immensely contributed to our understanding of alternative economic methodologies, the manner in which they have been conceptualized have also tended to reproduce Eurocentric notions of economics as a discipline. For example, one of the most striking implicit assumptions underlying much of the discussion on the "great divide" is that all of the most consequential debates surrounding economic theory occurred within the confines of Europe (Dobb 1975; Bharadwaj 1986). Yet from a historical perspective, this misses how theories and ideas that we take for granted today as quintessentially western

DOI: 10.4324/9781003316084-2

were in reality born out of a process of global connectedness and cultural percolation across regions. This is as true of economics as it is of other disciplines. Some of the most consequential categories and concepts that we consider central to contemporary development economics were products of a two-way cultural diffusion between the European and non-European worlds. One can cite the fact that the earliest conceptions of socialist utopias of 16th-century European thinkers "were dependent above all on the seminal contribution of Andean rationality to the new European imaginary that was being constituted" (Quijano 1993: 142); or the fact that Quesnay's attack on mercantilism in *Tableau Economique* was deeply influenced by Chinese thinking on political economy (Hobson 2004). In fact, even the labour theory of value had antecedents in the writings of Arab thinkers like Ibn Khaldun (Banaji 2007). These are but a few examples of how the non-western world co-produced key dimensions of what we consider classical (European) political economy today. Effacing these historical linkages has constrained the boundaries of economics, especially within the heterodox camps, and has led to a paradoxical situation where, on the one hand, heterodox economists have emphasized the importance of inclusivity and pluralism but, in practice, have largely failed to acknowledge the crucial contributions of thinkers from the Global South.[1] This blinkered history has had important theoretical consequences as well, which brings us to the second issue. The distinction drawn between production- and exchange-centric approaches has tended to elude the fact that both sides of the divide have historically shared a common conceptualization of capitalism as a closed economic system (Patnaik 2008). With the exception of Marx, who developed a partial framework on the link between capitalist reproduction and imperialism, both production-centred thinking and exchange-centred thinking have largely ignored the centrality of imperialism, despite the fact that historically speaking, capitalism has never existed in isolation from non-capitalist social formations.

In this chapter, we take this glaring lacuna as our starting point and argue that it is necessary to bring imperialism back into the heart of development thought. This requires not merely a reconstruction of what Patnaik (2008) calls the "propertyist" tradition of Marx, Keynes and Kalecki but also a bold cross-fertilization between propertyism and the anti-imperialist writings that have emerged from thinkers from the peripheries over the last century or so. Marxism, of course, has been a central convergence point for anti-imperialist thought, but neither Marx nor his "propertyist" successors have, after all, developed a full-fledged theory of imperialism, and the most prolific thinking on this front has emerged from thinkers outside the advanced capitalist societies (Williams 1945; Amin 1990; Naoroji 1996; Prebisch 1959). It is with this in mind that this chapter seeks to show how two of the most outstanding thinkers from the Global South sought to do precisely what thinkers like Marx had hinted at but had not been able to accomplish in their lifetime, namely explicitly theorize and understand how world-system-level forces govern the process of accumulation. The chapter focuses on the writings of Dadabhai Naoroji (1825–1917) from India and Raúl Prebisch (1901–1986) from Argentina in a comparative framework and outlines their innovative analysis of the problems of underdevelopment.

Unlike mainstream economic thought, which has historically emphasized the virtues of markets and in the process has forwarded a theoretical framework that divorces the accumulation process from the historical specificities of social formations, the writings of these thinkers from Asia and Latin America highlight the necessity of undertaking a structural analysis of the forces that fashioned the accumulation process (Mehmet 2002; Hodgson 2001; Sirohi 2017). They viewed the process of development holistically as a collective, societal process and emphasized the interdependent and cooperative nature of economic activities. Displacing the apolitical and individualized conception of progress based on competition and material gain, these voices stressed the socially embedded nature of accumulation (Leiva 2008). In this, they not only drew heavily on European intellectual traditions but also sought to modify them to the realities of the developing world by highlighting the negative effects of globalization and emphasizing how world-system-level dynamics shaped the economic fortunes of developing countries. By doing so, these thinkers sought to unshackle development discourse from its methodological internalism, which hid the complex, multi-scalar interplay of local and global forces that governed development (Kvangraven 2021). It is towards these contributions that we turn in the subsequent sections.

"The Grand Old Man of India": Naoroji and the Drain Theory

Dadabhai Naoroji belonged to the first generation of Indian nationalists, and his critique of colonial rule in India laid the intellectual basis for the subsequent anti-colonial movement that emerged in the sub-continent in the early decades of the 20th century (Patel 2020; Gandhi 2009). Apart from his influence within India, his writings played a crucial role in shaping the works of thinkers like Paul Baran (1957), and through him "the Indian debate on dependency could have had an impact on the Latin American debate" as well (Hettne 1983: 254). What made Naoroji's writings so influential in those days and what gives them their abiding relevance even today is that they run contrary to a central line of thought running through much of Western development literature since the 18th century about the civilizing potential of imperialism and the diffusion of development, especially in the form of "exports of capital" from advanced centres of capitalism to its peripheries (Hume 1987; Hilferding 1910; Hobson 2018; Warren 1980; Harvey 2003, 2007). It is, of course, true that in the writings of Adam Smith, Edmund Burke and other notable Irish nationalists and colonial administrators, there were hints about colonial tributes and the associated drain of wealth from colonies to metropoles, but as Bagchi

(1996) has noted, these incipient formulations were all but effaced from the 19th- and early 20th-century western economic discourse.[2] The result of this was that although European thinkers came to perceive the significance of the age of imperialism, the discussions remained centred on processes unfolding within Europe, with the colonies appearing merely as backcloths.[3]

The first and perhaps most influential 20th-century European writer to have brought attention to North-South capital exports was Rudolph Hilferding in his path-breaking study, *Finance Capital*, written a few years before the outbreak of the War (Hilferding 1910). In it, he identified the emergence of large banks and their fusion with industrial interests, which increasingly took the form of giant corporations, as the defining feature of European capitalism at the turn of the century. These transformations entailed a new stage in capitalist development because they marked a shift from the previous system of relatively free competition to one in which few large entities backed by massive banks dominated production. These structural changes, he argued, also gave rise to a new trend of capital exports from the developed world to the colonies. Whereas prior to the period of finance-led capitalism, it was trade in goods that dominated international transactions, the emergence of giant corporations in the advanced core changed this scene dramatically. Not only were these large corporations now able to establish foreign subsidiaries, but the sheer volume of capital that they handled also drove them to constantly find new avenues to invest capital in faraway lands. These exports were expressions of heightening contradictions, inter-European conflicts and so on, but they had a progressive side to them for the recipient economies in the sense that capital exports were seen as harbingers of progress in the non-Western peripheries.

It is worth emphasizing that Hilferding was not alone in underscoring the importance of capital exports, as this was a widely held assumption that many of his contemporaries shared at that time. Yet what this view missed was that while there were indeed voluminous capital exports being made from leading capitalist economies like Britain, these investments were primarily directed to areas of white settlement in North America, Australia and so on (Clemens and Williamson 2000; Nurkse 1954). Further, what was striking about these capital exports was that they were funded by political tributes that were extracted from colonies in Southern regions (Bagchi 2002; Patnaik 2006, 2013; Banerji 1982; Saul 1960). Thus far from being recipients of capital, the colonies were sources of capital that funded capitalist diffusion to the regions of white settlements in North America, Australia and so on. India was a crucial pivot in this triangular system. In 1880, its trade surpluses with the rest of the world were estimated to have covered a third of Britain's deficit, and by 1910, the figure stood at approximately 40% (Saul 1960). Put differently, according to a recent estimate, in the six-decade period from 1837–1838 to 1900–1901 alone, more than half a billion pounds were expropriated from India by its colonial rulers (Patnaik and Patnaik 2021).[4] Thus, not only was there little net export of capital from Britain to colonies like India, but on the contrary, it was capital surpluses siphoned off from the latter that fed industrial engines in Britain and other emerging centres of the Western Hemisphere. This was precisely what a number of anti-colonial writers were pointing to when they complained about the "drain" of wealth from India (Naoroji 1996; Dutt 2013a, 2013b; Ranade 2014b).

Now, the existence of a political tribute was hotly debated by the time Naoroji came on the scene, but it is worth emphasizing that during the early days of British rule, the existence of this tribute was openly noted by several English observers, and the term "drain" regularly appeared in many writings of colonial bureaucrats (Ganguli 1965; Sen 1992). In the early days of rule, the tribute mechanism was rather transparent and left little to the imagination. The East India Company monopolized land revenue that was earlier under the control of Mughal rulers and syphoned it off to Britain in commodity form. As one observer put it in 1787,

> the company are merchants as well as sovereigns of the country. In the former capacity they engross its trade, whilst in the latter they appropriate the revenues. The remittances to Europe of revenues are made in the commodities of the country, which are purchased by them.
>
> (Sir John Shore cited in Ganguli 1965: 89)

Thus, between 1750 and 1797, even as imports from India doubled, its exports grew slowly to 9 percent of total British exports from 6.4 percent in 1750 (Habib 1975). But with the shifting tides of the global economy and with changes within Britain itself, the role of India also underwent major transformations in the latter half of the 19th century (Mukherjee 2010). The British policy of discriminatory tariffs combined with meagre state support for domestic producers in India decimated local textile production and opened its markets up to British manufacturers. As India started to emerge as a large absorber of British manufacturing, its deficits with Britain increased. But even as this happened, concomitantly its trade surpluses with the United States and other newly emerging nations piled up, and these surpluses now became the centre of Britain's tribute realization (Sen 1992). The transfer of tributes remained very much like earlier in the sense that a part of locally raised revenues was set aside for "expenditure abroad", or what was during the days of the East India Company referred to as "investment", and this tribute was realized into sterling-denominated revenues by mopping up India's export surpluses in the name of payments for good British governance, termed "Home Charges" (Sen 1992; Patnaik 2013). But the crucial change now was the mechanism that enabled Britain to drain these resources, which involved a complex multi-lateral trading system and new financial instruments in the form of the "council bills" that were introduced in 1861. The "council bills" issued by the Secretary of

State in England and completely purchasable in foreign currencies in effect monetized India's trade surplus with the rest of the world. As Patnaik puts it:

> The foreign importers purchased bills (termed 'council bills') issued by the Secretary of State by paying in sterling and other currencies up to the value of their imports. The crucial characteristic of the bills was that they were encashable only in rupees – this was the feature designed to deny exchange earnings to the colonized producers. The sterling, US dollars, francs and other currencies given as payment by the rest of the world for India's net exports thus piled up in London, and the rupee bills issued against these sums were sent by the foreign importers to the Indian export-ers (by post or by telegraph) for encashing through local exchange banks; these rupees in turn came out of the sums earmarked in the Indian budget for that purpose, under the general head of expenditures incurred abroad.
>
> (Patnaik 2013: 13)

One of the earliest thinkers to have recognized the link between India's abnor-mally large export surpluses and the drain of wealth was Dadabhai Naoroji.[5] More than just a nationalist critic of British policies, Naoroji was an eminent economic analyst with original views and innovative thoughts. Unlike liberal readings of colonial India, which emphasized free markets and the benefits of comparative advantage, Naoroji (1996: 46–54) insisted that categories and theories of European political economy, while suitable to study the realities of Europe, had to be sufficiently modified when translated into colonial contexts before deploying them there. This view of course was widely shared by oth-ers and was best exemplified by Mahadev Govind Ranade (2014b: 324), who emphasized the need to contextualize economic theories and modify them ac-cording to "time and place and circumstances, the endowments and aptitudes of men, their habits and customs, their laws and institutions and their previ-ous history". Of particular significance to Ranade was the presumed juridical equality between contracting parties and the free flow of competitive forces that adherents of liberal political economy took for granted. While these as-sumptions may have had some basis in the Western context, in colonies such as India, they bore little resemblance to a social reality where caste, status, power and the political dynamics of imperialism all added together to create a complex web of economic, political and cultural hierarchies (Ranade 2014b: 328, 343; 2014a: 271). In such contexts, it was monopoly, force and relations of domination that governed the dynamics of accumulation, not the free, in-visible hands of the market.

These principles also govern the realm of international trade. For almost a century, it had become a truism to say that free trade between nations was ben-eficial to the world and to all parties involved. Yet what this text book version missed was that world trade in reality was neither free nor fair (Naoroji 1996, 1887b, c). In the system that had emerged over the 18th and 19th centuries, colonial powers dominated the world system, set its rules and even as they elevated the principles of free trade in rhetoric, they did everything in their power to reduce colonies to being mere appendages to their industries. Thus far from the abstract world of political economy, "free trade between England and India . . . is something like a race between a starving, exhausting invalid, and a strong man with a horse to ride on" (Naoroji 1996: 54).

In this British-dominated international trading regime, according to Naoroji, it was extra-economic compulsion that drove trade. Britain was able to use its political dominance over the sub-continent to siphon off the earnings from the export surpluses that the country had been able to accumulate on its external balances. In the name of a long list of "home charges", which included, apart from other things, pensions and remunerations of British officials in India, Indian export earnings were retained by its colonial masters and thus remained unrequited (Naoroji 1887c: 113–116). These export surpluses, combined with all the profit margins that the colony had to forgo on them, constituted one way of estimating the political tribute and, hence, a drain of wealth from the Indian economy to the British one (Naoroji 1996). As Dutt (2013b: 159) would later put it, it was the "great disproportion between the imports and the exports of British India" through which "Great Britain exacted a tribute from India for which she made no commercial return".

It is worth pointing out that for Naoroji, the export surplus represented only a fraction of the drain, as it did not take into account the fact that India's imports were captive in the sense that they included British-made goods that government stores purchased as a matter of policy, as well as all those British goods imported by European colonialists due to their Europeanized tastes and preferences (Naoroji 1996: 32). Moreover, the drain also had to include the profits earned by British firms, which had monopolized shipping trade and insurance (Naoroji 1996: 32). Thus, export surplus was at best a signpost and most definitely an underestimation of what was truly being taken away from the economy. In an 1867 intervention, using available parliamentary records, Naoroji (1887a) attempted to construct a more comprehensive estimate of the drain. Using available information, he constructed a series on the revenue "charges in India" and "charges in England". Assuming all "charges in England" were destined for Britain and setting aside one-eighth of "charges in India" (as an estimate for all the private remittances, government store purchases of British goods and so on), he calculated the total outflow of capital to be around £488 million between 1829 and 1865. For the period 1787–1829, he assumed one-tenth of the total "charges in India" were destined for Britain, which amounted to £60 million. Adding rough estimates of the tribute for the period and after making various concessions and assumptions, he concluded that the tributes drained between 1787 and 1865 were to the order of £1,600 million.

It was precisely this "price" for British rule that India was having to pay for, which, according to Naoroji (1887d), explained why its economy had stagnated, why famines had crippled the countryside, and why despite all its wealth, its citizens remained in dire poverty. In other words, the causes of underdevelopment were not to be found in missing institutional prerequisites but in the fact that part of the surplus generated from within the economy was drained away to the metropole. By emphasizing the political dominance of Britain as the cause of India's poverty, he sought to demolish the myth that colonialism benefited the Indian peoples and to show how hollow British claims of colonialism being a civilizing mission actually were. And it was this perspective that Naoroji and the generation of nationalists that he inspired extended to their politics as well.

Latin American Structuralism: The Ideas of Raúl Prebisch

Naoroji played a pivotal role in forging the Indian nationalist movement. He was one of the founders of the Indian National Congress in 1885, and he extensively toured Europe, where he built up a network of support for Indian "home-rule" demands (Patel 2020). Naoroji, however, was a moderate at heart. Even as he brought to focus the grinding poverty of the masses and, in some instructive passages, even noted the growing inequalities in his colonial society, his theoretical proclivities were not in any sense radical (Naoroji 1887b: 103). He focused his intellectual efforts on highlighting the adverse effects of foreign rule and believed that if the colonial rulers could be convinced of their follies and if India's bleeding could be put to an end, the root causes of its terrible poverty could be adequately addressed. But it was precisely in this political moment that his theorizing also revealed its glaring omissions and weaknesses. Taken to its logical end, the nationalist critique implied that the anti-colonial movement ought to "confine itself to questions in which the entire nation has a direct participation, and it must leave the adjustment of social reforms and other class questions to class Congresses" (Naoroji 1887e: 336). Thus, in its insistence on equating Indian underdevelopment with Britain's political dominance and by focusing its lens on the drain of wealth, what this perspective missed was that underdevelopment was far knottier than what this critique presumed because it functioned not only through colonially regulated external trade but also through the social and institutional framework rooted in society. It functioned, for example, through the laws and institutions promulgated by the colonial state, the lopsided patterns of land distribution, and social norms and arrangements like the dreadful caste system that predated colonial rule (Ambedkar 2016). Underdevelopment with the squalor and poverty it entailed was therefore more than just a result of the loss of political control that colonialism entailed it was a deeply ingrained coloniality that spread its tentacles in multifarious ways, and thus defeating it required more than just political independence; it required thoroughgoing structural reforms aimed at overturning the very structure of the colonial economic base, eliminating not just colonial oppression but unfreedoms of all other kinds that had bogged the country down and kept its people in chains. But it was precisely this "structural" reading of imperialism that was elided over by the nationalists like Naoroji and was thus taken to task by anti-caste radicals like Ambedkar, social reformers like Ranade and communists like M.N. Roy, who insisted that the critique of Britain's colonial policies be extended to a critique of class inequalities and to the structures of social oppression as well (Ambedkar 2016; Ranade 2014a; Roy 1944).

Now it is interesting to note that this "structuralist" understanding of imperialism *a la* Roy, Ambedkar and Ranade has a striking parallel in Latin America. Perhaps the earliest and most influential of these names was José Carlos Mariátegui, the Peruvian Marxist who, as we shall see in Chapter 2, produced some of the most incisive writings on imperialism in the early 20th century. Just like Naoroji, he noted the salience of the drain in Peru's external balance and pointed to how "The European nations have 'invisible importations' that equalize their commercial trade balance", but that "in Peru as in all countries with colonial economies, there are 'invisible exports'" which "mostly go outside the country in the form of dividends, interest, etc." (Mariátegui 2011a: 115). But of great importance to him was the fact that imperialism in Latin America was far more resilient and thus had a far wider connotation than just the imposition of alien political rule. Nations across Latin America had, after all, gotten their independence in the early 19th century, and yet despite formal political sovereignty, they remained economically dependent on foreign markets and foreign sources of capital (Mariátegui 2011b). The tentacles of imperialism therefore continued to spread throughout the region even after formal colonialism ended, and the fact that they were able to do so was because Latin American political independence did nothing to break the institutional framework that it inherited from its past and did little to change the economic ties that bound it to the world system. Any study of imperialism and any attempt to forge an anti-imperialist political strategy therefore had to recognize that its reproduction relied on more than just the political domination of one country over another (Mariátegui 2011). The perpetuation of imperialist ties relied fundamentally on a matrix of coloniality, which worked not only at the global level to drain resources from peripheries but also through cultural, economic and social structures within society as well (Quijano 2000, 2007).

The Latin American variant of "structuralism", which originated in the writings of thinkers like Mariátegui, came into its own and flourished in the post-War period (Pinto 2016; Sunkel and Girvan 1973; Furtado 2016; Cardoso and Faletto 1979). It drew on a number of influences ranging from Marxism to Keynesianism, but it was the Anglo-Saxon structuralist school that played an important role in its evolution (Sanchez-Ancochea 2007). The "high development theory"[6] associated with figures like Albert Hirschman (1958), Rosenstein-Rodan (1961) and Ragnar Nurkse (1971), amongst others, was a reaction to the orthodoxies of neoclassical economics. Whereas the latter equated development with specialization and global division of labour, these structuralists gave priority to inter-sectoral and inter-industrial linkages and hence division of labour within an economy (Ho 2016). Eschewing the methodological individualism of neoclassical theories, structuralists emphasized complementarities, externalities and the importance of coordination between individual firms, industries and sectors. Thus, development was not visualized as a sequence of successive stages in which underdeveloped countries had to first acquire a specific set of missing components before taking off on their development journey; rather, they saw it as "a process of drawing together a variety of conditionally available resources and latent abilities" (Hirschman 1958: 7; Lin and Monga 2017). Above all, successful development requires that linkages be built between various actors and that complementarities between their actions be magnified through public policies. There were, of course, differences between how these thinkers proposed these linkages be built, with some insisting on simultaneous, across-the-board investments across crucial sectors and others emphasizing unbalanced development in which key sectors would be given a lead role to play. But these differences notwithstanding, the common vision of development as a process that involved stage skipping, constant disequilibria and inter-sectoral articulation was a common theme in these writings.

Another crucial commonality between these thinkers was the relatively benign view they took of the international arena. Even Nurkse (1961, 1954), who was otherwise very conscious of the limits of export-led, foreign-finance-led development, nonetheless did not ever focus on the effects of global asymmetries on the development of poor countries. The global division of labour thus appeared as a backdrop to the process of development. It was here that Latin American structuralism, while building on the themes proposed by Western theorists, also sought to incorporate into them the salience of core-periphery dynamics (Sanchez-Ancochea 2007). The most celebrated structuralist explanations were the ones associated with Raúl Prebisch.[7]

Prebisch not only focused his analysis on the category of economic surplus in a classical political economy mould but also sought to move beyond the traditional closed system assumptions that underlay it by emphasizing the international forces that shaped it (Leiva 2008). He viewed social surplus as a historically specific category determined by the techniques of production, the power relations between contending classes, state policies and world-system-level dynamics. The techniques of production determined the size and composition of the social product at any given time, while the share of labour in the total social product determined the necessary consumption of society (Prebisch 1980: Part I, 1976; Prebisch 1981). The residual over and above this necessary consumption reflected the quantity of surplus left over for reinvestment in the economy, or, as he put it, "surplus consists in that part of the fruits of technical progress which is not transferred to the labour force because of the great heterogeneity of the periphery's socioeconomic structure" (Prebisch 1978: 167).

In placing weight on social surplus, Prebisch can be clearly placed within the so-called production-centred approach to economic development that can be traced back to William Petty, Adam Smith, David Ricardo and Karl Marx (Garegnani 1984). But there were three important differences between his analysis and the classical schema. First, in determining the social surplus, classical predecessors took wages, output and techniques of production as pre-given. The structural core of the classical schema consisted solely of economic variables because it was widely accepted that capitalist reproduction was driven by impersonal market forces alone and that, thus, there existed a strict institutional separation between political and economic spheres within capitalism (Cesaratto and Bucchianico 2021). None of this, of course, meant that the classical tradition ignored political and social forces in its analysis. Quite to the contrary, they placed these at the centre of their analysis, but as far as the study of surplus formation was concerned, these broader political dynamics were considered too complex to draw generalizations about and were thus left outside the theoretical core of analysis (Martins 2013).[8] Prebisch (1985: Part II, 1976: 14–17) in part followed the classical lead and noted how the share of wages tended to be relatively low in peripheries due to the existence of vast reserves of labour languishing in low-productivity activities; he also emphasized the active element by suggesting that wage shares, while shaped by structural forces, were ultimately variable and determined by the conflict between economic elites and working classes. In peripheral economies where democratization and trade union consciousness had taken root at a relatively early stage of development, workers often won important rights and thus often managed to shift distribution in their favour. The elites, for their part, did not remain passive bystanders. They reacted to such victories by bidding up prices to win back their income shares, and if that did not work, they utilized the brute force of state power to crush labour and bring wages back down to acceptable levels dictated by their profitability (Prebisch 1985: 68–69; 1976:17–18).[9] This meant that the structural core of Prebisch's schema included not only all those core variables identified by Garegnani (1984) but also extra-economic forces that shaped surplus formation.

A second aspect of Prebisch's definition of social surplus and perhaps the most distinguishing feature of his analysis was his emphasis on how surplus formation was governed by a country's position in the international hierarchy (Prebisch 2016, 1959).[10] Even in the absence of formal colonial links, Prebisch noted that international trade functioned in such a way as to drive surpluses from the agricultural South to the industrial North (Ocampo and Parra-Lancourt 2010; Love 1980). The reason for this, he argued, stemmed both from the low-income elasticities of primary commodity exports from the South and structural differences between developed and developing nations, because of which the developed world not only managed to keep the purchasing power of its exports intact but, over the long run, even improved it vis-à-vis the largely agrarian periphery (Baer 1962). More precisely, unlike the developed world, where productivity differences across sectors had more or less equalized, in the developing world, economies were characterized by dualistic structures (Prebisch 1959: 254–261). In the "modern" export-oriented sector, productivity was determined by global linkages and was thus exogenously driven. The rate of growth of output in the modern sector was constrained by the limited nature of external demand and thus typically lagged behind productivity growth. The overall result was therefore a tendency for workers to be shed from the export-oriented "modern" sector, resulting in a constant tendency for the overall pool of labour reserves in the "traditional" sector to expand. This perennially expanding surplus labour tended to keep wages depressed, and prices in the South thus remained downwardly flexible. By contrast, labour markets in advanced cores were comparatively tighter due to structural homogeneity and the fact that workers there were typically better organized to protect their wages. This fact made it so that prices were downwardly rigid in these developed parts of the world. As Prebisch (2016: 55) explained it:

> During the upswing, part of the profits are absorbed by an increase in wages, occasioned by competition between entrepreneurs and by the pressure of trade unions. When profits have to be reduced during the downswing, the part that had been absorbed by wage increases loses its fluidity, at the centre, by reason of the well-known resistance to a lowering of wages. The pressure then moves toward the periphery, with greater force than would be the case if, by reason of the limitations of competition, wages and profits in the centre were not rigid. The less that income can contract at the centre, the more it must do so at the periphery.

This brings us to the third and final point. Classical political economists and even Marx, who was otherwise extremely critical of the social effects of capitalism, all held onto a heroic imaginary of capitalism as a revolutionizing, productive force. As Marx and Engels (2007: 12) put it in the *Communist Manifesto*,

> the bourgeoisie cannot exist without constantly revolutionizing the instruments of production, and thereby the relations of production, and with them the whole relations of society. . . . Constant revolutionizing of production, uninterrupted disturbance of all social conditions, everlasting uncertainty and agitation distinguish the bourgeois epoch from all earlier ones.

Whatever the role of the bourgeoisie was in Europe, as far as Prebisch was concerned, the story was quite different in the peripheries. Prebisch argued that the problem of underdevelopment in Latin America stemmed not just from an inadequacy of surplus but also from the fact that the narrow cabal of elites that appropriated social surplus tended to fritter it away on ostentatious consumption of goods imported from abroad rather than investing them into productive ends (Prebisch 1976: 11–12; 1980:182, 1985: 65), leading to "a considerable waste of capital accumulation potential, with which is combined the siphoning-off of income by the centres -especially through the transnational corporations-, thanks to their technical and economic superiority and their hegemonic power" (Prebisch 1980: 156). Here, there was a stark contrast between Naoroji and Prebisch. Whereas the former largely focused on the negative effects of the drain, Prebisch also emphasized the distribution of surplus and pointed to how social heterogeneities impacted the accumulation process; in other words, the problems of underdevelopment, for the Latin American structuralists, arose as much from an insufficiency of surplus as from the manner in which existing surpluses were utilized.

Bringing Imperialism Back Into Development Debates

To sum up our discussion, some final comments are in order. There has been an unfortunate tendency in mainstream economics to gloss over the thorny question of imperialism, and what is even more striking is the fact that this kind of blindness has also been characteristic of radical heterodox traditions as well. Thus, for instance, some of the most influential critiques of mainstream, neoclassical economics that have emerged in the last few decades fail to mention the question of imperialism, let alone raise it as a core concern around which heterodox economics ought to be built (Hodgson 2001; Keen 2011; Lee and Jo 2011). Marxists, especially those in the West, too, have not had a better record on this matter. The works of Wood (2005), Callinicos (2009) and Harvey (2003, 2007) are good examples of how the study of "new" imperialism has completely effaced traditional concerns of self-determination and anti-colonialism as found in the writings of Marx himself but also of Lenin and scores of anti-imperialist thinkers from the South (Sirohi and Bhupatiraju 2021). This is despite the fact that the Marxist framework has been a crucial pole around which a number of anti-imperialist thinkers from the Global South have consistently rallied. This blindness, it is important to add, is not merely an innocent happenstance but rather a result of a very specific set of assumptions that have dogged Western economic thought. The classical, production-centric thinkers, including Marx, focused their analysis on the forces that governed social surplus formation. Surplus was considered to be that portion of social output that was left over after covering the necessary consumption of society. It represented all the means that were available to society to enhance productive powers, diversify the economic base and acquire new and more complex capabilities (Garegnani 1984). By training lenses on social surplus, adherents of this approach highlighted the necessity of undertaking a structural-institutional analysis of the forces that fashioned the accumulation process. But also worth repeating here is the fact that in the writings of classical political economists and their radical heir, Marx, one finds, despite several differences, a common conceptualization of capitalism as a closed economic system; a system that, based on its own bootstraps, is able to reproduce and propel itself forward (Patnaik 2006). In other words, there was an implicit view that surplus formation, distribution and its ultimate allocation amongst various ends were governed by forces that were internal to capitalist social formations. Thus, even as the European empire expanded across the globe and even as industrialization at home became indispensably linked to slavery, colonial markets and the latter's primary commodities, the link between capitalist reproduction at home and the global web of colonial ties abroad was never really given much weight in the writings of the early production-centric thinkers (Bhambra 2020). Associated with this methodological internalism was a heroic imaginary of capitalism as a totalizing unity whose forward march was seen as being so powerful as to transform far-flung peripheries in the image of Europe (Chakrabarty 2008).

Marx, especially towards the end of his life, had become less sanguine about the globalizing potential of capitalism, and as many of his lesser-known writings suggest, he was able to develop a rich, non-teleological view of the non-Western world (Habib 1998; Anderson 2010). Although there are no known records of him having ever met his contemporary, Dadabhai Naoroji, who frequently travelled to Britain, it is likely that the two crossed paths, and it has been temptingly suggested that Marx's late writings on the Indian colonial situation may have been influenced by Naoroji's work (Patel, 2015). It is interesting to note that Naoroji's own classic book of 1901 was published by Swan Sonnenschein & Co., which also published Volume I of Marx's *Capital* (Habib 1998). Further, they shared a common acquaintance in the British socialist, Henry Hyndman.[11] Shortly after Hyndman had come across Naoroji's writings, he wrote to Marx in 1881, indicating that he wished for them to meet (Patel 2015). Whether or not they actually met is not known, but subsequent to Hyndman's letter, Marx (1968) noted in a correspondence to Nikolai Danielson, that:

> What the English take from them [India] annually in the form of rent, dividends for railways useless to the Hindus; pensions for military and civil service men, for Afghanistan and other wars, etc., etc. – what they take from them without any equivalent and quite apart from what they appropriate to themselves annually within India, speaking only of the value of the commodities the Indians have gratuitously and annually to send over to England – it amounts to more than the total sum of income of the sixty millions of agricultural and industrial labourers of India! This is a bleeding process, with a vengeance!

Yet Marx's writings on colonialism were fragmentary and never fully developed. Those who took on his mantle in the early 20th century, including figures like Lenin, produced a large corpus of writings on the centrality of imperialist ties between oppressor and oppressed nations, which unfortunately have all been rendered invisible by contemporary economic thinking. It is precisely here that the views of Naoroji and Prebisch acquire great importance. They emphasized, in their own ways, the centrality of economic surplus as a core category of analysis, and in this they can be firmly placed within the production-centred approach to development. But they also produced innovative and original interventions that broke with the territorial container that the surplus discourse had been stuck in. Where traditionally global dynamics were seen as inconsequential in the generation of social surplus, Dadabhai Naoroji and Raúl Prebisch placed global relations at the centre of their analysis. Both noted the salience of global power asymmetries and emphasized how these global dynamics shaped the size, composition and utilization of the social surplus in developing countries. While Naoroji understandably was far more focused on the insufficiency of surplus stemming from India's external drain, Prebisch, writing at a different time, was able to develop a far more nuanced, multi-scalar description of surplus formation and its relation to the multi-faceted problems of underdevelopment in Latin American economies.

Focusing our attention on global dynamics as asserted by Prebisch and Naoroji is essential not only to recuperate the bold visions of these two Southern thinkers but also because their views are strikingly relevant even today, and this is what makes a comparative study between the two a useful and worthwhile project to undertake. The contemporary world economy has no doubt undergone major transformations over the last century or so, and the prospects of development in the Global South today are no longer what they were in the days of Naoroji. The globalization of finance, the splintering of manufacturing across the developed world, and the rise of emerging economies in Asia, Africa and Latin America mark a new phase of global capitalist development. Despite these massive shifts, it is important to note that there remain sharp continuities that link the past and the present (Sirohi and Bhupatiraju 2021; Ince 2014). Outright colonialism may be a thing for the history books, but the global landscape continues to be shaped by stark asymmetries. Thus, even as several countries within the Global South have been able to acquire new technological capabilities, "the number of non-western countries which have become developed is less than ten" (Wade 2014: 3). Viewed from a longue durée, the story of development has therefore been one of "divergence, big time" (Pritchet 1997). Notwithstanding the "tectonic shift of industry to the periphery, the basic conditions of center and periphery continue in most cases to hold" (Foster 2015), as evidenced by the massive transfers of surpluses from developing regions to advanced centres of the world economy in the neoliberal era (Hickel *et al.* 2021; Ricci 2018; Rice 2007). Thus, even as emerging nations have seen rapid industrial development, this has come to be associated not so much with the eclipse of imperialism as with the emergence of a new kind of imperialism (Suwandi 2019; Smith 2016). It is precisely here that the intersections between surplus formation, its realization, its distribution and world-system-level dynamics remain as relevant today as they did back then. The writings of Naoroji and Prebisch have resounding relevance as they provide rich frames to theorize these multi-scalar entanglements.

Notes

1 As an example, in recent years there has been much introspection about the past, present and future of heterodox economic approaches (Hodgson 2019; Potts 2021). Debates have focused on the methodological lacunae within heterodox approaches and have impressed upon the need to address theoretical gaps. Strikingly, there is very little discussion on issues of imperialism and colonialism or on the importance of recognizing intellectual contributions from the non-Western world. This is an issue that has been raised in some recent works and deserves greater attention than is currently afforded (Bhambra 2020; Kvangraven and Kesar 2022; Kvangraven 2023). For an incisive discussion on the methodological lacunae in political economy traditions, see Bagchi (1996).

2 For a discussion on the Irish political economy school, see Rashid (2018, 2021)

3 Lenin's writings, especially after 1915, and Rosa Luxemburg's studies on imperialism were exceptions in many senses. Lenin, of course, largely took over Hobson and Hilferding's thesis on the export of capital but never truly succumbed to their Eurocentric excesses. This would become abundantly clear after 1917 in his radical positions on the national question (Blaut 1997). Similarly, Rosa Luxemburg, in a celebrated pamphlet titled *What is Economics?* published posthumously, noted the large export surpluses that colonies were compelled to maintain vis-à-vis the metropoles (Luxemburg 1970). This was, as we shall see, Naoroji's central assertion. It is worth emphasizing that Naoroji attended the Second International in 1904, where he rubbed shoulders with luminaries of the socialist movement, including Rosa Luxemburg (Habib 1998; Patel 2020).

4 There are several other estimates. See, for instance Maddison (2010), Cuenca-Esteban (2007) and Bagchi (2002)

5 Naik (2001) notes that prior to Naoroji, the drain theory's basic foundations were already being discussed by Indian radicals who wrote both in English and regional languages.

6 Krugman (1993)

7 Amongst a long list of honours, Prebisch was the recipient of the Jawaharlal Nehru Award for International Understanding in 1974.

8 The idea of separating the analysis of the "pure" economy as distinct from institutional analysis was formalized by Luigi Pasinetti and has come to be known as the "separation theorem" (Pasinetti 2021).

9 Prebisch's argument has parallels with the profit-squeeze theory that had become popular in the 1980s and argued that the ongoing capitalist crisis stemmed from increasing wages (Sherman 1984; Gordon *et al.* 1987). This has also been a continuing theme in the writings of "new developmentalists" like Bresser-Pereira (2006).

10 Hans Singer (1949, 1950) independently developed similar arguments.

11 Hyndman belonged to a generation of British socialists who were sympathetic to anti-colonial struggles in India. Hyndman founded the Social Democratic Federation of England and developed close ties with Indian nationalists like Naoroji, Tilak and Lajpat Rai, amongst others. He was a critic of British colonial policies, and his writings in popular media regularly referred to the drain of wealth from India. His article titled "The Bankruptcy of India", which first appeared in 1878, called attention to the "tremendous economical drain" imposed on the colony and its consequences for the Indian people (Hyndman 1878).

References

Ambedkar, B. R. (2016). *Annihilation of Caste: The Annotated Critical Edition.* New Delhi: Navayana Publishing.

Amin, S. (1990). *Delinking: Towards a Polycentric World.* London: Zed Books.

Anderson, K. B. (2010). *Marx at the Margins: On Nationalism, Ethnicity, and Non-Western Societies.* Chicago: University of Chicago Press.

Baer, W. (1962). The Economics of Prebisch and ECLA. *Economic Development and Cultural Change,* 10 (2), 169–182.

Bagchi, A. K. (1996). Colonialism in Classical Political Economy: Analysis, Epistemological Broadening and Mystification. *Studies in History,* 12 (1), 105–136.

Bagchi, A. K. (2002). The Other Side of Foreign Investment by Imperial Powers: Transfer of Surplus from Colonies. *Economic and Political Weekly,* 37 (23), 2229–2238.

Banaji, J. (2007). Islam, the Mediterranean and the Rise of Capitalism. *Historical Materialism,* 15 (1), 47–74.

Banerji, A. K. (1982). *Aspects of Indo-British Economic Relations, 1858–1898.* Bombay: Oxford University Press.

Baran, P. A. (1957). *The Political Economy of Growth.* New York: Monthly Review Press.

Bhambra, G. K. (2020). Colonial Global Economy: Towards a Theoretical Reorientation of Political Economy. *Review of International Political Economy,* 28 (2), 307–322.

Bharadwaj, K. (1986). *Classical Political Economy and Rise to Dominance of Supply and Demand Theories,* 2nd edition. New Delhi: Orient Longman.

Blaut, J. M. (1997). Evaluating Imperialism. *Science and Society,* 61 (3), 382–393.

Bresser-Pereira, L. C. (2006). The New Developmentalism and Conventional Orthodoxy. *Économie appliquée,* 59 (3), 95–126.

Callinicos, A. (2009). *Imperialism and Global Political Economy.* Cambridge: Polity.

Cardoso, F. H. and Faletto, E. (1979). *Dependency and Development in Latin America.* Berkley and Los Angeles: University of California Press.

Cesaratto, S. and Di Bucchianico, S. (2021). The Surplus Approach, Institutions, and Economic Formations. *Contributions to Political Economy,* 40 (1), 26–52.

Chakrabarty, D. (2008). *Provincializing Europe: Postcolonial Thought and Historical Difference.* Princeton, NJ: Princeton University Press.

Chang, H. J. and Andreoni, A. (2021). Bringing Production Back Into Development: An Introduction. *European Journal of Development Research,* 33 (2), 165–178.

Clemens, M. A. and Williamson, J. G. (2000). *Where Did British Foreign Capital Go? Fundamentals, Failures and the Lucas Paradox: 1870–1913,* NBER Working Paper No. 8028, Cambridge, Mass.: National Bureau of Economic Research.

Cuenca-Esteban, J. (2007). India's Contribution to the British Balance of Payments, 1757–1812. *Explorations in Economic History,* 44 (1), 154–176.

Dobb, M. (1975). *Theories of Value and Distribution Since Adam Smith: Ideology and Economic Theory.* Cambridge: Cambridge University Press.

Dutt, R. C. (2013a). *The Economic History of India Under Early British Rule; From the Rise of the British Power in 1757 to the Accession of Queen Victoria in 1837.* London: Routledge.

Dutt, R. C. (2013b). *The Economic of History of India in the Victorian Age: From the Accession of Queen Victoria in 1837 to the Commencement of the Twentieth Century,* London: Routledge.

Engerman, S. L. and Sokoloff, K. L. (2005). *Colonialism, Inequality, and Long-run Paths of Development*, NBER Working Paper No. 11057, Cambridge, Mass.: National Bureau of Economic Research.

Foster, J. B. (2015). The New Imperialism of Globalized Monopoly-finance Capital: An Introduction. *Monthly Review*. retrieved from: https://monthlyreview.org/2015/07/01/the-new-imperialism-of-globalized-monopoly-finance-capital/ [viewed 15/08/23].

Furtado, C. (2016). Development and Underdevelopment. In R. Bielschowsky (Ed.), *Thinking: Selected Texts, 1948–1998*. Santiago De Chile: ECLAC, 141–148.

Gandhi, M. K. (1908 [2009]). *Hind Swaraj*. In A. Parel (Ed.), *M. K. Gandhi: Hind Swaraj and Other Writings*. Cambridge: Cambridge University Press, 1–126.

Ganguli, B. N. (1965). Dadabhai Naoroji and the Mechanism of 'External Drain'. *The Indian Economic and Social History Review*, 2 (2), 85–102.

Garegnani, P. (1984). Value and Distribution in the Classical Economists and Marx. *Oxford Economic Papers*, 36 (2), 291–325.

Gordon, D. M., Weisskopf, T. E. and Bowles, S. (1987). Power, Accumulation, and Crisis. In R. Cherry, C. D'Onofrio, C. Kurdas, T. R. Michl, F. Moseley, and M. I. Naples (Eds.), *The Imperilled Economy: Macroeconomics from a Left Perspective*. New York: Monthly Review, 43–58.

Habib, I. (1975). Colonialization of the Indian Economy, 1757–1900. *Social Scientist*, 32 (3), 23–53.

Habib, I. (1998). The Left and the National Movement. *Social Scientist*, 26 (5/6), 3–33.

Harvey, D. (2003). *The New Imperialism*. Oxford: Oxford University Press.

Harvey, D. (2007). *A Brief History of Neoliberalism*. New York: Oxford University Press.

Hettne, B. (1983). The Development of Development Theory. *Acta Sociologica*, 26 (3/4), 247–66.

Hickel, J., Sullivan, D. and Zoomkawala, H. (2021). Plunder in the Post-Colonial Era: Quantifying Drain From the Global South Through Unequal Exchange, 1960–2018. *New Political Economy*, 26 (1), 1–18.

Hilferding, R (1910). *Finance Capital: A Study of the Latest Phase of Capitalist Development*. Retrieved from: www.marxists.org/archive/hilferding/1910/finkap/index.htm [Viewed 23/3/2023]

Hirschman, A. O. (1958). *The Strategy of Economic Development*. New Haven: Yale University Press.

Ho, P. S. W. (2016). Linking the Insights of Smith, Marx, Young and Hirschman on the Division of Labour: Implications for Economic Integration and Uneven Development. *Cambridge Journal of Economics*, 40 (3), 913–939.

Hobson, J. M. (2004). *The Eastern Origins of Western Civilisation*. Cambridge: Cambridge University Press.

Hobson, J. A. (2018). *Imperialism: A Study*. London: Routledge.

Hodgson, G. M. (2001). *How Economics Forgot History: The Problem of Historical Specificity in Social Science*. London: Routledge.

Hodgson, G. M. (2019). *Is There a Future for Heterodox Economics? Institutions, Ideology and a Scientific Community*. Cheltenham: Edward Elgar Publishing.

Hume, D. (1987). *Essays: Moral, Political, and Literary*. Edited by E. F. Miller. Indianapolis: Liberty Classics.

Hyndman, H. (1878). The Bankruptcy of India I, *Nineteenth Century*, 4 (20), 585–608. Retrieved from: www.marxists.org/archive/hyndman/1878/10/bankruptcy-india-1.htm [Viewed 23/03/2023]

Ince, O. U. (2014). Primitive Accumulation, New Enclosures, and Global Land Grabs: A Theoretical Intervention. *Rural Sociology*, 79 (1), 104–131.

Keen, S. (2011). *Debunking Economics. The Naked Emperor Dethroned?* London: Zed Book.

Krugman, P. (1993). *The Fall and Rise of Development Economics, Mimeo*. Cambridge, MA: MIT.

Kvangraven, I. H. (2021). Beyond the Stereotype: Restating the Relevance of the Dependency Research Programme. *Development and Change*, 52 (1), 76–112.

Kvangraven, I. H. (2023). The Need to Centre Imperialism. In C. O. Christiansen, M. L. Machado-Guichon, S. Mercader, O. B. Hunt, and P. Jha (Eds.), *Talking about Global Inequality*. Cham: Palgrave Macmillan, 81–87.

Kvangraven, I. H. and Kesar, S. (2022). Standing in the Way of Rigor? Economics' Meeting with the Decolonization Agenda. *Review of International Political Economy*, 1–26.

Lee, F. S. and T. H. Jo. (2011). Social Surplus Approach and Heterodox Economics. *Journal of Economic Issues*, 14 (4), 857–875.

Leiva, F. I. (2008). *Latin American Neostructuralism: The Contradictions of Postneoliberal Development*. Minneapolis: University of Minnesota Press.

Lin, J. Y. and Monga, C. (2017). *Beating the Odds: Jump-Starting Developing Countries*. Princeton, NJ, and Oxfordshire: Princeton University Press.

Love, J. L. (1980). Raúl Prebisch and the Origins of the Doctrine of Unequal Exchange. *Latin American Research Review*, 15 (3), 45–72.

Luxemburg, R. (1970). What is Economics?. In Mary-Alice Walters, (ed), *Rosa Luxemburg Speaks*, (pp. 219–249), Pathfinder Press, New York.

Maddison, A. (2010). *Class Structure and Economic Growth: India and Pakistan since the Moghuls*. New York: Routledge.

Mariátegui, J. C. (2011). Anti-Imperialist Viewpoint. In H. E. Vanden, and M. Becker (Eds.), *José Carlos Mariátegui: An Anthology*. New York: Monthly Review Press.

Mariátegui, J. C. (2011a). Colonial Economy. In H. E. Vanden and M. Becker (Eds.), *José Carlos Mariátegui: An Anthology*. New York: Monthly Review Press, 122–123.

Mariátegui, J. C. (2011b). Peru's principal problem. In H. E. Vanden and M. Becker (Eds.), *José Carlos Mariátegui: An Anthology*. New York: Monthly Review Press, 126–129.

Martins, N. O. (2013). Classical Surplus Theory and Heterodox Economics. *American Journal of Economics and Sociology*, 72 (5), 1205–1231.

Marx, K. (1968). *Marx to Nikolai Danielson in St. Petersburg* . In *Marx and Engels Correspondence*. New York: International Publishers. Retrieved from: www. marxists.org/archive/marx/works/1881/letters/81_02_19.htm [Viewed 28/4/23].

Marx, K. and Engels, F. (2007). *Manifesto of the Communist Party*. New York: International Publishers.

Mehmet, O. (2002). *Westernizing the Third World: The Eurocentricity of Economic Development Theories*. London: Routledge.

Mukherjee, A. (2010). Empire: How Colonial India Made Modern Britain. *Economic and Political Weekly*, 45 (50), 73–82.

Naik, J. V. (2001). Forerunners of Dadabhai Naoroji's Drain Theory. *Economic and Political Weekly*, 4428–4432.

Naoroji, D. (1887a). England's Duties to India. In C. L. Parekh (Ed.), *Essays, Speeches, Addresses and Writings (on Indian Politics) of the Hon'ble Dadabhai Naoroji*. Bombay: Caxton Press, 26–50.

Naoroji, D. (1887b). Wants and Means of India. In C. L. Parekh (Ed.), *Essays, Speeches, Addresses and Writings (on Indian Politics) of the Hon'ble Dadabhai Naoroji.* Bombay: Caxton Press, 97–111.

Naoroji, D. (1887c). On the Commerce of India. In C. L. Parekh (ed.), *Essays, Speeches, Addresses and Writings (on Indian Politics) of the Hon'ble Dadabhai Naoroji.* Bombay: Caxton Press, 112–136.

Naoroji, D. (1887d). Memorandum No. 2, The Moral Poverty of India, and Native Thoughts on the Present British Indian Policy. In C. L. Parekh (Ed.), *Essays, Speeches, Addresses and Writings (on Indian Politics) of the Hon'ble Dadabhai Naoroji.* Bombay: Caxton Press, 464–479.

Naoroji, D. (1887e). Inaugural Address: Second Indian National Congress. In C. L. Parekh (Ed.), *Essays, Speeches, Addresses and Writings (on Indian Politics) of the Hon'ble Dadabhai Naoroji.* Bombay: Caxton Press, 331–344.

Naoroji, D. (1996). *Poverty and Un-British Rule in India.* 2nd edition. New Delhi: Publications Division, Ministry of Information and Broadcasting, Government of India.

Nurkse, R. (1954). International Investment To-Day in the Light of Nineteenth-Century Experience. *The Economic Journal,* 64 (256), 744–758.

Nurkse R. (1961). International Trade Theory and Development Policy. In H. S. Ellis (Eds.), *Economic Development for Latin America.* London: Palgrave Macmillan, 234–274.

Nurkse R. (1971). The Theory of Development and the Idea of Balanced Growth. In A. B. Mountjoy (Eds.), *Developing the Underdeveloped Countries. Geographical Readings.* London: Palgrave Macmillan, 115–128.

Ocampo, J. A. and Parra-Lancourt, M. (2010). The Terms of Trade for Commodities Since the Mid-19th Century. *Revista de Historia Económica/Journal of Iberian and Latin American Economic History,* 28 (1), 11–43.

Pasinetti, L. L. (2021). Economic Theory and Institutions. *Structural Change and Economic Dynamics,* 56, 438–442.

Patel, D. (2020). *Naoroji: Pioneer of Indian Nationalism.* Cambridge, Mass.: Harvard University Press.

Patnaik, P. (2008). *The Value of Money.* New Delhi: Tulika Books.

Patnaik, U. (2006). The Free Lunch: Transfers From the Tropical Colonies and Their Role in Capital Formation in Britain During the Industrial Revolution. In K. S. Jomo (Ed.), *Globalization Under Hegemony: The Changing World Economy.* New Delhi: Oxford University Press, 30–70.

Patnaik, U. (2013). India, the Great Depression and Britain's Demise as World Capitalist Leader. In B. Dasgupta (Ed.), *External Dimensions of an Emerging Economy, India: Essays in Honour of Sunanda Sen.* Abingdon: Routledge, 7–28.

Patnaik, U. and Patnaik, P. (2021). The Drain of Wealth Colonialism before the First World War. *Monthly Review,* 72 (9), 1–22.

Pinto, A. (2016). Nature and Implications of The "Structural Heterogeneity" of Latin America. In R. Bielschowsky (Ed.), *ECLAC Thinking: Selected Texts, 1948–1998.* Santiago De Chile: ECLAC, 303–314.

Potts, J. (2021). How Heterodox Economics Lost Its Way. *Journal of Economic Issues,* 55 (3), 590–594.

Prebisch, R. (2016). Economic Development of Latin America. In R. Bielschowsky (Ed.), *ECLAC Thinking: Selected Texts, 1948–1998.* Santiago De Chile: ECLAC, 45–84.

Prebisch, R. (1959). Commercial Policy in the Underdeveloped Countries. *The American Economic Review*, 49 (2), 251–273.

Prebisch, R. (1976). A Critique of Peripheral Capitalism. *CEPAL Review*, 1, 9–76.

Prebisch, R. (1978). Socio-economic Structure and Crisis of Peripheral Capitalism. *CEPAL Review*, 6, 159–252.

Prebisch, R. (1980). Towards a Theory of Change. *CEPAL Review*, 10, 155–208.

Prebisch, R. (1981). Dialogue on Friedman and Hayek: From the Standpoint of the Periphery. *CEPAL Review*, 15, 153–174.

Prebisch, R. (1985). The Latin American Periphery in the Global Crisis of Capitalism. *CEPAL Review*, 26, 63–88.

Pritchett, L. (1997). Divergence, Big Time. *Journal of Economic Perspectives*, 11 (3), 3–17.

Quijano, A. (1993). *Modernity, Identity, and Utopia in Latin America*. Boundary 2, 20 (3), 140–155. https://doi.org/10.2307/303346.

Quijano, A. (2000). Coloniality of Power, Eurocentrism, and Latin America. *Nepantla: Views from South*, 1 (3), 533–580.

Quijano, A. (2007). Coloniality and Modernity/Rationality. *Cultural Studies*, 21 (2–3), 168–178.

Ranade, M. G. (2014a) Industrial Conference. In B. Chandra (Ed.), *Ranade's Economic Writings*. Delhi: Gyan Publishing House, 269–279.

Ranade, M. G. (2014b) Indian Political Economy. In B. Chandra (Ed.), *Ranade's Economic Writings*. Delhi: Gyan Publishing House, 322–349.

Rashid, S. (2018). From Anxiety to Nonchalance: 'Neoclassical Economic Development' From 1950 to 2000. *History of Political Economy*, 50 (S1), 286–302.

Rashid, S. (2021). *Archbishop King's Some Observations on Taxes, and the 'Colonial Drain'*. Mimeo: Rashid. Retrieved from: https://ssrn.com/abstract=3808135

Ricci, A. (2018). Unequal Exchange in the Age of Globalization. *Review of Radical Political Economics*, 51 (2), 225–245.

Rice, J. (2007). Ecological Unequal Exchange: Consumption, Equity, and Unsustainable Structural Relationships Within the Global Economy. *International Journal of Comparative Sociology*, 48 (1), 43–72.

Rosenstein-Rodan P. N. (1961). Notes on the Theory of the 'Big Push'. In H. S. Ellis (Eds.), *Economic Development for Latin America*. London: Palgrave Macmillan, 57–81.

Roy, M. N. (1944). *Planning a New India*. Calcutta: Renaissance Publishers.

Sanchez-Ancochea, D. (2007). Anglo-Saxon Versus Latin American Structuralism. In E. Pérez Caldentey and M. Vernengo (Eds.), *Ideas, Policies and Economic Development in the Americas*. New York: Routledge, 208–226.

Saul, S. B. (1960). *Studies in British Overseas Trade, 1870–1914*. Liverpool: Liverpool University Press.

Sen, S. (1992). *Colonies and Empire: India 1870–1914*. Calcutta: Orient Longman.

Sherman, H. J. (1984). Inflation, Unemployment, and the Contemporary Business Cycle. In J. B. Foster, and H. Szlajfer (Eds.), *The Faltering Economy*. New York: Monthly Review Press, 91–117.

Singer, H. W. (1949). Economic Progress in under-developed Countries. *Social Research*, 16 (1), 1–11.

Singer, H. W. (1950). The Distribution of Gains Between Investing and Borrowing Countries. *American Economic Review*, 40 (2), 473–485.

Sirohi, R. A. (2017). Colonial 'Shock' and Global Inequalities: A Critical Review of New Institutional Economics. *Economic & Political Weekly*, 52 (33), 85–93.

Sirohi, R. A. and Bhupatiraju, S. (2021). *Reassessing the Pink Tide: Lessons From Brazil and Venezuela*. Singapore: Palgrave Macmillan.

Smith, J. (2016). *Imperialism in the Twenty-First Century: Globalization, Super-Exploitation, and Capitalism's Final Crisis*. New York, NY: Monthly Review Press.

Sunkel, O. and Girvan, C. (1973). Transnational Capitalism and National Disintegration in Latin America. *Social and Economic Studies*, 22 (1), 132–176.

Suwandi, I. (2019). *Value Chains: The New Economic Imperialism*. New York, NY: Monthly Review Press.

Wade, R. (2014). *Industrial Policy—Better, Not Less*. Paper Presented at UNCTAD Trade and Development Board Sixty-first session, Geneva. Available at: https://unctad.org/meetings/en/Presentation/tdb61_Rwade_item8_en.pdf [Viewed 15/08/23].

Warren, B. (1980). *Imperialism: Pioneer of Capitalism*. London: New Left Books.

Williams, E. (1945). *Capitalism and Slavery*. Chapel Hill: University of North Carolina Press.

Wood, E. M. (2005). *Empire of Capital*. London and New York: Verso.

2 Development and Social Identities

Race and Caste in Mariátegui and Ambedkar[1]

This chapter juxtaposes the radical legacy of two great thinkers of the Global South, José Carlos Mariátegui (1894–1930) from Peru, and Bhimrao Ramji Ambedkar (1891–1956) from India, focusing on their ideas on race and caste in the articulation of their socialist vision and exploring their contemporary relevance for the emancipatory projects of our times.

Despite mounting empirical evidence, development thought has largely ignored the linkages between social identities and the process of capital accumulation. The most celebrated neoclassical growth models, for instance, have paid little heed to race or caste, despite the fact that the entire history of capitalist development has been inextricably linked to segregated labour markets. Absent from any theoretical framework, caste- or race-based disparities have been brushed off as individualized phenomena with little or no connection to the fundamental forces that drive capitalist accumulation. But, as discussed in the previous chapter, the entire tradition of production-centred economic thought, which has tended to take social classes as their starting point of analysis, has also left questions of social identities to the margins of its analysis. This has had a considerable effect not only on how heterodox scholars and academicians have come to see social identities but also on how radical political movements have come to see social identities. The rise of identity-based movements since the early 1980s, for example, has generated considerable debate within left/emancipatory politics as to the nature and origins of such movements and, more importantly, as to the stance to be adopted vis-à-vis their politics (Karat 2011; Fraser 2000; Harvey 2014; Wood 2000; Hobsbawm 1996). In contrast to the universalistic appeals that animated much of leftist politics in the 20th century, the explosion of identity-based movements, with their emphasis on social experiences of exclusion and their prioritization of identitarian agendas rather than class interests, has created a deep sense of unease within the left, to the extent that large sections now view identity politics as a handmaiden of neoliberal capitalism (Karat 2011; Reed 2013, 2018). In some senses, it is not difficult to see why such reactions are so widely prevalent, as there have been numerous instances of identity-based movements clashing directly with traditional

DOI: 10.4324/9781003316084-3

left parties and their programmes (Reed 2018). But more than just these scattered examples, at the heart of the left's discomfort with identity politics is its own long-held identification with the historical materialist critique of capitalism, which sees class struggle and class exploitation as the fundamental loci of political action. As one influential interpretation puts it, capitalism "is uniquely indifferent to the social identities of the people it exploits", so much so that "there is a positive tendency in capitalism to *undermine* such differences, and even to dilute identities like gender or race" (Wood 2000: 266). As a result,

> if capital derives advantages from racism or sexism, it is not because of any structural tendency in capitalism toward racial inequality or gender oppression, but on the contrary because they disguise the structural realities of the capitalist system and because they divide the working class.
>
> (Wood 2000: 267)

Identity politics from this perspective falls short because even as it "claims a unique sensitivity to the complexities of power and diverse oppressions . . . it has the effect of making invisible the power relations that constitute capitalism" (Wood 2000: 261). It follows from this that the demands for recognition can be completely compatible with the continued reproduction of capitalism with all its horrors and inequities.

Such critiques that have emerged over the last decade or so have raised enormously important political concerns and served as potent correctives to culturalist excesses that have come to the forefront in the neoliberal years. But in doing so, there has also been a tendency on their part to reduce matters to rigid binaries, thereby ceding too much ground to those voices who claim that there is a fundamental incompatibility between left politics grounded in historical materialism and the pursuit of social reform as championed by identity-based movements.[2] The causal priority of class that the left asserts is, of course, completely in line with the precepts of historical materialism, and this assertion is a necessary check against the "culturalist turn" that has become fashionable in recent years. Yet, interpreted too mechanically, it can become a terrible guide to praxis especially in the context of the Global South. "One of the basic principles of dialectics", Lenin reminds us, "is that there is no such thing as abstract truth, truth is always concrete" (Lenin 1904: 409). And in the concrete realities of contemporary developing economies, there is no denying that race, caste or gender continue to hold incredible sway on how societies and economies are structured (Robinson 2000; Bhattacharyya 2018). Further, even if these identities are assumed to be, as Wood and others suggest, inconsequential to the logic of capital at a certain level of abstraction – though this is not the only possible interpretation of historical materialism[3] – to derive from this an axiomatic prioritization of one kind of struggle over another is to miss the close links between reform and revolution. Such a position can only hurt the ability of the left/emancipatory projects to spread its/their wings amongst the poorest and most oppressed layers of society.

The most problematic aspect of the class-identity binary that is being drawn up today is, therefore, its effect on the political strategy of the left. The tendency to reject culturalist assertions has led many on the left, particularly in India, to a blanket rejection of many legitimate complaints raised by identity-based movements, and this has alienated precisely those sections of society that ought to have been its natural allies. What is even more striking is that such devaluations of identity concerns run completely contrary to the revolutionary legacy of socialist movements and anti-colonial struggles. Despite the widely held view that "Traditional Marxist formulations of the abstract categories of class cannot address the specificity of group identities such as the indigenous, the poor, racialized peoples, women, religious minorities, and sexual minorities", Marx and Engels, by the end of their lives, had developed a very nuanced perspective on issues of nationalism, racism and gender oppression (Alcoff 2011: 72; Anderson 2010). What was a subterranean theme with Marx and Engels was brought out into the open by Lenin. As the first major worker's revolution broke out in Eastern Europe, it was this towering figure no less who brought to the forefront of global Marxist discourse the salience of the rights of minorities and the right of nations to self-determination (Harding 1983; Anderson 2007). His interventions paralleled heated discussions and debates within what is today known as the Global South, where there were numerous attempts by Marxists and non-Marxists alike to creatively incorporate issues of gender, race and other identity markers into the very heart of anti-colonial theory and practice (Prashad 2017).

It is in this context that this chapter seeks to highlight how these two revolutionary thinkers of yesteryear, who were also contemporaries, sought to theorize the social realities that they confronted in their immediate surroundings. The following sections describe how both of these radical thinkers foregrounded issues of race and caste, respectively, in the context of rising nationalist/anti-colonial tides and in the context of militant class struggles that had started to emerge in both regions. The chapter delineates the similarities and differences in the way each thinker theorized the intricate links between social oppression, class struggle and imperialism. The comparative analysis raises questions that remain of great relevance to socialist politics even today.

To put this comparative study in a broader academic perspective, we may note that the interconnectedness of race and caste has occasioned significant scholarship that has examined parallel experiences of marginalization of Blacks and Dalits in their locational specificities. The linkages established between the Pan-African struggle against racial segregation and the Dalit struggle against untouchability are based on the recognition of race and caste as markers of oppressed identities (Slate 2012; Pandey 2010, 2013). Given this context, studies on race and caste as "comparable systems of oppression" (Reddy 2005: 545) have mainly juxtaposed African and African-American racial experiences with those of the disenfranchised Dalits in South Asia. By contrast, the trajectories of racial capitalism in Latin America have been conspicuously absent from the comparative framework they employ, except in sporadic instances. A study juxtaposing Mariátegui and Ambedkar as thinkers from two outposts of the Global South can therefore additionally serve as an attempt to fill this gap and add to the recent renewal of interest in comparing racism and casteism as two salient forms of social exclusion.

Race, National Liberation and Class Struggle: José Carlos Mariátegui's Creative Marxism

Mariátegui was one of the most prolific writers to have emerged in early 20th-century Latin America. Founder of the Peruvian Socialist Party in 1928, he

> was clearly and irrevocably committed to both socialism and the defense of Indigenous rights. He challenged *indigenista* intellectuals who, critiquing the Indian reality from a privileged educated and urban perspective, asserted that racial inferiorities lay at the heart of their poverty.
>
> (Becker 2006: 453)

Mariátegui instead stressed that the marginalization of the country's indigenous population had to be first and foremost understood in the context of the highly unequal economic structure of Latin American societies, especially the lopsided patterns of land ownership (Mariátegui 2011g). The "socialist point of view" required that the indigenous question be seen "as a fundamentally economic problem", as opposed to the "instinctive and defensive tendency of the *creole* or *mestizo* to reduce it to a purely administrative, pedagogical, ethnic, or moral problem" (Mariátegui 2011a: 66). Here he saw an intricate link between racial slavery, the class structure of Peru and the larger dynamics of the capitalist world-system (Webber 2015; Kay 2011; Helleiner and Rosales 2017).

Born in 1894 in the small town of Moquegua, Mariátegui suffered a debilitating injury as a child, one that would dog him for the rest of his life until his death in 1930.[4] The injury prevented him from attending school, but what he missed in terms of formal education he made up through voracious reading. Such was his intellectual promise that, as a teenager, he readily found work as a journalist in *La Prensa*, a leading newspaper in Lima. It was here that Mariátegui came into close contact with the leading artists, intellectuals and political activists of his generation. Lima, during the early decades of the 20th century, was at the centre of a cultural and political effervescence. The Bolshevik Revolution had a major influence on him, and in 1919, he co-founded with César Falcón the newspaper *La Prensa,* whose socialist orientation was clear in the support it lent to a wide variety of political movements, ranging from the anarcho-syndicalist trade unions to the university reform movement, which, beginning in Argentina in 1918, would go on to spark off important political changes in many Latin American countries, including Peru. New literary groups like the *Colónida,* which Mariátegui was associated with, sprung up around this time and gave artistic expression to the mass disenchantment that had gripped Peruvian society (De Castro 2020). They critiqued what they perceived as a longstanding intellectual subservience to the West and called for new directions and models in literature. The *Colónidas* "were, for Mariátegui, rebellious iconoclasts, dissident members of their class, antibourgeois pursuing new artistic directions, new imaginative expressions that would be, perhaps, artistic anticipations of a new reality" (Gonzalez 2019: 38). Influenced by these diverse currents, Mariátegui's early writings on art and culture already started to exhibit a tinge of unconventionality, and his militant journalism brought him into direct confrontation with the government of the day, which exiled him and his associate César Falcon to Europe. It was during his stay in Europe that he came to see first-hand militant working class movements and was introduced to Marxist-Leninist ideas that had an enormous influence on him.[5] The bohemian was transformed into a radical, and by the time of his return to Peru in 1923, he had come to self-identify as a Marxist. But the Marxism that he held dear was a Marxism that was flexible, free of dogma and a guide to action. Mariátegui was greatly influenced by Lenin, and like him, his revolutionary practice was informed by the material conditions obtaining in his country (Noakes 2021:9). He believed that Marxism had to be creative:

> Marxism, of which all speak but few know or above all comprehend, is a fundamentally dialectic method. It is a method that is completely based in reality, on facts. It is not, as some erroneously suppose, a body of principles of rigid consequences, the same for all historical climates and all social latitudes. Marx extracted his method from history's guts. Marxism, in every country, in every people, operates and acts on the environment, on the medium, without neglecting any of its modalities.
>
> (Mariátegui 2011e: 157)

In the context of Peru and Latin America more generally, creative Marxism required placing the issue of imperialism at the centre of analysis. The region's economic dependency and the consequent marginalization of the indigenous communities, he noted, had deep historical roots that went back to its colonial experiences. Columbus's arrival in the "New World" in 1492 inaugurated the rise of capitalism in Europe and began what was to become a long and irreversible subjugation of South America. In the decades that followed Columbus's voyage, the Spanish Crown gained control over the main centres of the Aztec and Incan empires and used its dominant position to pump out vast amounts of wealth from its American colonies (Galeano 1997). The new

European rulers, Mariátegui noted, "had a rather exaggerated idea of the economic value of natural wealth, but almost no idea about any of the economic value of people" (Mariátegui 2011a: 70). The Spanish saw in their colonies only a vast resource base to exploit and saw in its inhabitants a vast pool of labour to enslave. By giving precedence to extraction rather than wealth creation, the colonizers "turned mining into a factor of annihilation of human capital and the decline of agriculture" (Mariátegui 2011a: 74). The production of this vast wealth, moreover, went hand in hand with a sweeping transformation of the local social arrangements that had underlay the pre-Hispanic order. The intricate mechanisms of tribute payments and inter-community exchange relations that had formed the base of the Amerindian empires were transformed under the Spanish into a brutal mechanism of primitive accumulation. The combined effects of these institutional changes, harsh working conditions and new epidemics brought by the Europeans led to a propitious decline in the Amerindian population. The Europeans "disrupted and annihilated the Incas' agricultural economy" but they did so "without replacing it with an economy of higher yields". Thus, whereas

> Under an Indigenous aristocracy, the natives made up a nation of ten million men, with an efficient and organic state who ruled all its territory. Under a foreign aristocracy the natives were reduced to a scattered and chaotic mass of a million men reduced to servitude and peonage.
>
> (Mariátegui 2011a: 70)

Therefore, in contrast to the caste system, which predated colonialism, racism in Latin America was a direct outgrowth of the exploitative relationship between indigenous communities and European rulers, which came about as a result of the colonial rupture.

Independence from colonial rule in the early 19th century ought to have liberated indigenous communities from the shackles placed on them by their erstwhile rulers, but the formation of a republic further "impoverished the Indians . . . compounded their depression and exasperated their misery" (Mariátegui 2011d: 126). As he saw it, the entire episode of independence did neither really involve the indigenous masses nor raise to the forefront any of their major demands and aspirations (Mariátegui 2011a, Mariátegui 2011d). Thus, while independence ended one type of domination, by its very elitist nature, it left untouched other forms of exploitation and oppression in society. White skin continued to remain an indispensable marker of social status, and as a counterpart to this, the indigenous population came to be viewed as "natural slaves", lacking any autonomy of their own and thus in need of tutelage (Wade 2010; Hale 1986). Thus, freedom from European masters, argued Mariátegui, merely announced the transition from one set of exploiters to another and the transition from one kind of economic dependence to another. More precisely, independence came at a time when the native bourgeoisie was weak and the social status of the older, aristocratic elites, whose wealth and power lay in their concentrated land holdings, was as yet intact. The combination of factors meant that in Peru and elsewhere, "Rather than a conflict between the landowning nobility and commercial bourgeoisie, in many cases the Latin American revolutions resulted in their collaboration" (Mariátegui 2011a: 79). Whereas in the European experience, the bourgeoisie emerged as a champion of innovation, a prophet of accumulation and a political hammer force directed against feudalism, in the context of Latin America, the incipient capitalist class, from the very beginning, had little incentive to push forward along this path. It sought at each step to compromise with the agrarian oligarchs at home and imperialist capital abroad (Mariátegui 2011f). Given the nature of Latin American independence, a characteristic feature of its society was the persistence of land inequalities and the continued sway of landlords in the countryside. Therefore, rather than breaking the bonds of colonial exploitation, independence led simply to the "ascent of a new ruling class", which monopolized land and marginalized Indians even more than their colonial predecessors (Mariátegui 2011d: 126).

In a context such as this, racism, imperialism and landlordism developed intricate connections (Helleiner and Rosales 2017). The native bourgeoisie in alliance with agrarian oligarchs had no interest in developing a sovereign economy and much rather preferred subordinating itself to imperialist capital because it perceived "cooperation with imperialism as the best source of profits" (Mariátegui 2011f: 231). Foreign capital, in turn, desired from Peru and other Latin American countries a steady flow of primary commodities that were demanded at home. But here was the crux: with several competing sources of primary goods, what foreign capital demanded the most of these countries was that these goods be provided on "favorable terms" (Mariátegui 2011a: 104). As Mariátegui stated it,

These markets see Peru as a primary product deposit and a market for their manufactured goods. Because of this, Peruvian agriculture only receives investment credit and transportation for the products that Peru offers to the big markets on favorable terms. Foreign finance is interested in rubber one day, cotton on another, and another day in sugar. The day that London can get a product at a better price from India or Egypt it will instantaneously leave its suppliers in Peru to their own fate.

(Mariátegui 2011a: 104)

In an economy where innovations and technical progress were far and few, these favourable terms rested on the ability of landlords, domestic capital and foreign capital to curtail wage costs. This is where the indigenous peasantry became crucial: they represented a pool of workers that could be ground, crushed and exploited to no end. Racism directed against the Indigenous population institutionalized the super-exploitation of these workers, thus cementing the relationship between race and peripheral capitalism. It was this that formed the fulcrum around which the alliance between domestic elites and foreign capitalists also functioned:

> For Yankee or English imperialism, the economic value of these lands would be much less if in addition to its natural resources it did not possess a backward and miserable Indigenous population that, with the assistance of the national bourgeoisie, it is possible to exploit to the extreme. . . . The work of enslaved peasant masses, housed in disgusting shanties, deprived of all freedoms and rights, subject to a backbreaking workday, placed Peruvian sugar planters in a position to compete with those in other countries who better cultivated their lands or were protected by a protective tariff or were better situated from a geographical point of view.
>
> (Mariátegui 2011g: 264–265)

In sum, therefore, Mariátegui viewed Latin America's principal problems as being intricately connected to the dependent insertion of the region into the Western dominated world-system. He saw imperialism not just as an economic condition but also as a condition of "coloniality" that extended to every pore of social life (Quijano 2000, 2007). The overarching influence of imperialism stunted the development of Peru, and both the country's bourgeoisie and its middle classes were complicit in the region's continued mental and material enslavement (Mariátegui 2011f). Unlike Haya de la Torre, a one-time ally of Mariátegui who believed that a reformed capitalism could be built by a movement led by the middle classes and the country's "national" bourgeoisie, Mariátegui "saw no scope for the development of an autochthonous or independent national capitalism" (Kay 2011: 17). Thus, the slogan of "Peruvianizing, nationalizing, emancipating" the country was achievable only through the agency of workers and peasants and not through some broad anti-imperialist front of the kind Haya de La Torre was seeking to build (Mariátegui 2011c: 123). The struggle for Peru's soul then had to be simultaneously socialist and anti-imperialist, but what was more, it also had to be anti-racist for it to hold any meaning in countries like Peru: "A policy that is truly national in scope cannot dispense with the Indian; it cannot ignore the Indian. The Indian is the foundation of our nationality in formation. . . . Without the Indian no Peruvianness is possible" (Mariátegui 2011d: 127–128).

The Indians with whom he identified nationhood were, however, not just passive objects of the impending socialist struggle. They were not the helpless community in need of philanthropy and upliftment that the *indigenista* intellectuals had in mind. In Mariátegui's view, they were quite the opposite: the prime bearers of the revolution in Peru, its revolutionary vanguard, its national liberator (Mosquera 2018). It was not just their own objective economic conditions that made the indigenous peasantry the most likely to take on this mantle but also its long-standing cultural traditions rooted in what he saw as "Inca communism", which fostered collectivist norms, social solidarity and modes of reciprocity, all of which aligned very well with the socialist perspective (Mariátegui 1971). Mariátegui was heavily influenced by romanticism, and his writings indicated a critical but profound appreciation of Andean traditions (Löwy 1998; Yountae 2017). On this count, Mariátegui, as many have noted earlier, took several liberties with Marxism (Mariátegui , 2011h). While he placed his historical analysis of Latin America in a materialist framework, his romanticism led him to emphasize the decisive role of ideas, myths and even religion (Löwy 1998; Webber 2015; Kim 2015; Angotti 1986).

Situating Caste: B.R. Ambedkar's Quest

Ambedkar came into the political limelight in the 1920s, a period that witnessed the emergence of a mass anticolonial movement in India. A prolific writer with degrees in law and political science from the United States and the United Kingdom, his forthright views on nationalism, his sharp and unorthodox style of writing, and his principled political activism not only earned him ardent followers within the country but also put him on a collision course with the leading lights of the nationalist movement. He, of course, shared with the mainstream nationalist movement a deep resentment against British rule, but this resentment he felt also had to be tempered by the fact that the oppression of the Dalits had its roots in an inhumane social order that was in place well before the British arrived. Centuries old, India's caste hierarchies were a system of "graded inequality" in which economic and cultural entitlements decreased the lower one went down the caste ladder; it was, as Ambedkar put it, "an ascending scale of hatred and a descending scale of contempt" (Ambedkar 2019: 96). The caste system's division of society into the pure and impure, into the upper and lower castes, invited comparisons with racism and the dynamics of class amongst several contemporary thinkers. But Ambedkar repeatedly stressed the peculiarities and novelties of the caste system. As opposed to those radicals who emphasized the racial origins of the caste system, Ambedkar was extremely reluctant to collapse the mechanisms of caste oppression into categories of racism, although he expressed his admiration and solidarity with the African American struggles for racial equality (Goyal 2019; Deshpande and Darity 2003). He likened the category of caste to that of "an Enclosed Class" and repeatedly stressed how caste hierarchies were far more rigid than even the most developed class divisions (Ambedkar 2014a: 15). At the most basic level, what set the caste system apart was that it was driven by a self-reinforcing oppressive logic: fall in line with social rules or risk being condemned as an outcaste. These hierarchies did not require courts and institutions to uphold them because they were enforced through the "quasi-juridical authority" of its holy book itself, which punished errant behaviour with social boycott and ostracism (Rao 2009). "This negative force held the caste order together, making structural violence integral to the molecular order of caste" (Rao 2009: 127).

The world that Ambedkar wanted to build and the vision of an independent India that he held dear till the very end of his life were those of a social order free of economic and social injustices. Just like Marx and Engels (2007: 31), who exhorted workers to fight for a new world where "In place of the old bourgeois society, with its classes and class antagonisms, we shall have an association, in which the free development of each is the condition for the free development of all", Ambedkar too defined his vision of an independent India in similar terms. His ideal social arrangement was one in which

> the individual is an end in himself and that the aim and object of society is the growth of the individual and the development of his personality. Society is not above the individual and if the individual has to subordinate himself to society, it is because such subordination is for his betterment and only to the extent necessary.
>
> (Ambedkar 2019: 81)

In such a social order, "terms of associated life between members of society must be regarded with consideration founded on liberty, equality and fraternity" (Ambedkar 2019: 81). It is worth stressing that, for Ambedkar, liberty here implied not just the ability of "doing what one likes to do" but also "effective power to do specific things" and that this positive kind of liberty could only be said to exist in a social order

> where exploitation has been annihilated, where no suppression of one class by another exists, where there is no unemployment, no poverty and where a person is free from the fear of losing his job, his home and his food as a consequence of his action.
>
> (Ambedkar 2019: 86)

Ambedkar's entire case for uprooting the caste system can even be seen as stemming from this quasi-Marxist vision of an independent India. The caste system and the *Laws of Manu* that legitimized it were impediments to the construction of a free social order because they were the very negation of a society seeking the all-round development of human potential. They entailed a regression from egalitarianism in a double sense in that they not only oppressed lower castes and denied them their humanity but they carried their "principle of graded inequality . . . into the economic field" as well (Ambedkar 2019: 104). Invoking Marx's *Critique of the Gotha Program*, Ambedkar stressed that instead of the principle "From each according to his ability; to each according to his need", what guided the Hindu social order was its exact opposite, namely, "From each according to his need. To each according to his nobility" (Ambedkar 2019: 104).

Given the intertwined fates of class and caste in the Indian context, Ambedkar was certain that there could be no separation of anti-caste demands from anti-capitalist ones. In keeping with this view, he actively supported popular struggles across his home state of Maharashtra and became involved in some of the biggest mass urban strikes in the state in the 1930s and 1940s. The Indian Labour Party founded by him similarly sought to build broad alliances between Dalit and non-Dalit workers and peasants. The manifesto of the party highlighted the differential experiences of low-caste labour, but it also cast its net wide by demanding state ownership of key sectors, compulsory education, tax reform, the provision of assistance to the landless and the unemployed and so on (Omvedt 1994). It is in this context that the tense relationship between Ambedkar and the Communist leadership must be seen as a paradox of sorts. That Ambedkar was treated shabbily by the largely upper-caste leadership of the Communist movement is a matter of historical record, and he in turn responded in kind (Teltumbde 2019; Omvedt 1994). But what is also clear is that Ambedkar, despite several reservations, felt deeply affiliated with Marxism: "With the exception of Rousseau, no other thinker could take Marx's place for Ambedkar" (Kumar 2015: 40). And yet, despite these striking convergences in worldviews, what put him on a collision course with the socialist leadership was the fact that, while he saw class as "an important- and even primary-prism through which to view and understand society, he did not believe it was the only one" (Roy 2015: 114). Unlike those voices that saw caste struggles as unimportant and ultimately divisive, Ambedkar's analysis led him to believe that in societies such as India's, the universalistic goals of socialism were impossible to achieve without first tackling the particularistic demands of anti-caste movements (Teltumbde 2018, 2019). The errors that the Indian socialists were making, he deduced, stemmed from their mechanical and uni-linear understanding of working-class consciousness (Ambedkar 2015). The objective position of toilers in a country like India no doubt created a common bond of solidarity, but the unity of the working class was something that could not automatically be read off from objective economic conditions alone. In a society where the virus of the caste system was so deeply ingrained, a revolutionary working class had to be constructed through political struggle. All those who sought to separate socialist politics from anti-caste struggles failed to realize just how morally pernicious and how terribly divisive the caste system was, and that without its complete annihilation, there was little hope for a united working class to join together for larger anti-systemic goals. For the caste system was "not merely a division of labour" it was in reality "*a division of labourers*" and, in some senses, even more divisive than that, because it constituted "a hierarchy in which divisions of labourers are graded one above the other" (Ambedkar 2015: 233–234, emphasis original). To ignore this as the socialists had done and to assume that caste consciousness, so deeply entrenched in Indian society, would somehow automatically evolve into class consciousness was not just unrealistic; it was downright harmful to the achievement of socialist goals. After all, "Men will not join in a revolution for the equalization of property unless they know that after the revolution is achieved they will be treated equally, and that there will be no discrimination of caste and creed" (Ambedkar 2015: 232).

If Ambedkar railed against the socialists, he was even more unforgiving of the Gandhi-led Indian National Congress (INC). Like Mariátegui, for whom the marginalization of the indigenous community in Peru was directly linked to its dependency on the West and who saw in the struggle for national liberation a key to advancing both anti-capitalist and anti-racist programmes, Ambedkar too perceived national liberation as a necessary precondition to Dalit emancipation. But given the peculiar nature of caste, he had a more complex take on the relationship between caste discrimination and imperialism (Guru 2016). In part, this was because he identified the "Hindu social order" rather than the *British Raj* as the driving force behind the violence of caste, but this view was also influenced by the mainstream nationalist movement's silence on caste reforms, which Ambedkar perceived as proof of its complicity in reproducing these social hierarchies (Guru 1998; Gaikwad 1998). From a historical perspective, the nationalist movement in India was a very peculiar one. Despite mass insurrections occurring on a scale that was rarely witnessed in the colonial world, these did not snowball into a peasant-led revolution as was the case with China. That these movements did not radicalize was to a large extent the failure of the left, but it was also the result of the uncanny political prowess of the INC and its phenomenally influential leader, Gandhi.

Formed in 1885, the INC started out as an organization representing the interests of the native middle class, a class that the British had consciously developed to be "Indian in blood and colour, but English in taste, in opinions, in morals, and in intellect" (Thomas Macaulay, cited in Maddison 2010: 41). Disgruntled with their lack of representation within the institutions of the *British Raj*, the INC was formed to provide a platform for these middle layers to press their grievances to the government and to forward their demands for greater representation within the political and institutional framework of the colonial state. Given the nature of its origins, the INC, from its very inception, distanced itself from radical demands for social and economic reforms. Even as workers and peasants across the country flocked towards it, the upper echelons of its leadership and its entire political orientation remained tightly tied to the interests and perspectives of upper-caste Hindus. Increasingly, the INC also attracted the support of the small but politically important native capitalist class, which only served to increase the divisions within it (Frankel 2005). In the short run, the INC sought to overcome these tensions by projecting itself as a "'supra-class' and secular organization, with a political program acceptable to all Indians, irrespective of region, religion, or social class" (Palat *et al.* 1986: 193). But the very caste-class basis on which its organization functioned meant that there were severe restrictions on what it was willing and not willing to do (Palat *et al.* 1986). One such restriction that the INC clearly set out was with respect to the demands made by the assertive Dalit movement for the abolition of the caste system.

It was precisely the populist kind of nationalist discourse that the Gandhi-led INC had been peddling that Ambedkar sought to problematize. The goal of his critique was not just to expose the failings of the *British Raj*; it was also to strip down the entire architecture of Indian society and expose the feebleness of nationalist demands for civilizational equality. For Ambedkar, freedom without equality was no freedom at all (Guru 2016). And while the British had done precious little for the betterment of the sub-continent during their century and a half of rule, they had introduced into a society that naturalized untouchability important Western liberal ideals like the "principle of equality before law" (Ambedkar 2014c: 146). In a highly unequal society such as that of India, where social laws were based on undermining the humanity of Dalit peoples, this seemingly small intervention "served as a great disinfectant"; it "cleansed the air" and constituted "a real gain to the Untouchables" (Ambedkar 2014c: 147). Ambedkar was by no means a crude diffusionist, and he certainly shared with the nationalist movement a deep antipathy towards British rule. But whereas the mainstream movement demanded that freedom from political domination take priority over all other concerns, Ambedkar repeatedly hammered home his contention that freedom would be meaningless unless it was enriched with a promise of social equality. Ambedkar was clear that the way out for the toiling Dalit masses was not to place their faith in the colonial government because the British could not be expected to do much more than make small symbolic gestures. Instead, Dalit masses had to fight for the construction of a democratic society where decision-making institutions were directly answerable to the toiling, hungry and socially oppressed majority (Ambedkar 2014b).

Oppression and Exploitation: Towards New Alliances and Dialogues

Mariátegui's and Ambedkar's writings on race and caste presented here provide rich frames to analyse and interpret the dilemmas faced by the left today. Both thinkers drew heavily from European intellectual traditions but were acutely aware that they were writing in the context of countries whose historical experiences were very different from those of the West. The peripheral status, the economic backwardness and the prevalence of sharp social stratification in their respective countries threw up new challenges that required innovative answers. Consequently, while both thinkers were inspired by Marxist ideas, they also believed that these ideas had to be reconstituted and rearticulated to the peculiar conditions of the countries where they lived. In short, Peruvian and Indian socialisms could not be an imitation of readymade models from abroad but had to be instead a "heroic creation" (Mariátegui 2011b: 87; 2011e). In keeping with these views, they sought to vernacularize Marxism, and their quest to incorporate issues of race and caste into the heart of revolutionary theory and practice was one such attempt.

The first striking feature of both thinkers is their insistence on placing the dynamics of race and caste in the broader context of the capitalist world-system. Given the colonial/dependent status of both regions at the time of their writing, both thinkers viewed national sovereignty as absolutely essential for constructing a free social order. Mariátegui, in particular, saw socialist goals as organically connected with Peru's national liberation. His emphasis on imperialism and his belief in the emancipatory potential of national liberation were reflective of a striking feature of the development of Marxist thought in the Global South in the early 20th century: whereas in Europe socialism came to the political limelight largely as a result of working-class-based movements, in the non-Western world, its trajectory was closely connected to yearnings for national liberation.[6] Starting from its translation into the Russian context and then onto its extensions on non-European sites,

> East Marxism as a body of theory came to see in the nation not simply a given framework within which the class struggle occurred, but the form and substance through which Marxist goals could be realised and in which they would be embodied.
>
> (Seth 1989: 287)

In this regard, Mariátegui's attempts to wrestle with issues of race and to draw out their connections with imperialism and the politics of national liberation represented one of the earliest and most original attempts to absorb Marxism within the Peruvian and Latin American contexts.

On this matter, Ambedkar converged considerably with Mariátegui. Ambedkar, like his Latin American counterpart, recognized the importance of national liberation and, just like him, was adamant that freedom from external dependence was merely a means to an end and that unless this freedom was enriching and supplemented by promises of social and economic justice, it would only end up as a farce. But Ambedkar was also writing in a very different context, as a representative of the Dalit minority pitted against a homogenizing nationalist movement that was seeking to incorporate the majority and the minority under a single umbrella. Moreover, unlike racism, which was an ascriptive categorization and which originated in the context of colonialism, caste was a very different animal whose origins dated far before India's integration into the global capitalist orbit (Deshpande and Darity 2003). Ambedkar, given his location, therefore saw in anti-imperialist movements a double-edged sword. In its invocations of nationalism, he clearly saw a resource for Dalit self-recognition and a platform for the subalterns to mark their presence as active agents of history (Guru 2016). But lurking within these calls for unity and their invocations of ancient civilizational oneness, they also carried with them the risk of completely whitewashing the violence of India's past and the risks of cultural homogenization and majoritarianism. Thus, whereas Mariátegui could invoke his country's pre-colonial past as a resource for building socialism, Ambedkar, as a representative of oppressed minorities, was far warier as he sought to balance the violent history of caste inequalities with the emancipatory potential of the parallel, competing historical traditions of India (symbolized by Buddhism), which he strongly felt could provide a crucial resource for Dalit struggles (Ambedkar 2003).[7]

Differences notwithstanding, both their views on the intersections of social oppression and imperialism have great relevance today. While there has been a tendency to underplay the relevance of imperialism in today's world economy, the fact remains that contemporary globalization has not so much transcended imperialist ties between the Global South and North as it has transformed them (Patnaik and Patnaik 2016). The massive spurt in global capital flows and the splintering of production across the globe notwithstanding, the world economy today continues to be marked by sharp inequalities and power differentials (Smith 2016; Lauesen and Cope 2015). And what is more is that just as earlier, the "new" form of imperialism that we are witnessing today has entailed a massive squeeze on Southern labour reserves, the brunt of which has been experienced by socially oppressed communities. Race, caste and gender have not just persisted in the era of globalization, but they have also in many ways become more deeply ingrained than ever before (Nathan and Kalpana 2007; Phillips 2013; LeBaron and Gore 2020; Roy Chowdhury and Abid 2022). We, of course, no longer have the national liberation movements of the kinds that raged in the early half of the 20th century, and even the language of nationalism has today largely been cornered by the right, which has emptied it of all egalitarian content, deploying it only to deepen imperialist penetration of the Global South (Sirohi 2019; Roy Chowdhury 2020). Sections of the left, in turn, have retreated to embracing an uncritical cosmopolitanism, which sees in nationalism at best a slogan that is passé and at worst an impediment to the progressive march of globalization (Hardt and Negri 2000). It is precisely here that Mariátegui's and Ambedkar's complex understanding of imperialism and national liberation becomes extremely relevant; while nationalism may have become a bad word for the left and nation-state-centred activism too old-fashioned, Mariátegui's and Ambedkar's views suggest a different, more provocative perspective is possible to imagine. Without romanticizing the nation state and keeping in mind all of the risks that nationalism carries with it, the voices of these two stalwarts suggest that they nonetheless may still serve as crucial, albeit contested, sites of action for the left to wage struggles for social reforms and economic redistribution.[8]

A second and important insight that follows from a comparative reading of these two writers is the innovative manner in which they theorized the connections between identity and class. This emphasis on linking class struggle with the struggle for social reforms stands in stark contrast to recent debates on the left. As we noted in the introduction, there has been a tendency today to divorce identity from class and to treat these as separate, dichotomous categories, with class in some senses being perceived as more "real" than caste or race. The justification for this usually tends to pivot on the definition of capitalism as a mode of production in which surplus value is extracted through purely market-based, economic means alone and where, as a result, the only identity of labouring masses that matters is that of "interchangeable units of labour abstracted from any specific personal or social identity" (Wood 2000: 211; Anievas and Nisancioglu 2014; Rioux 2013; Byrd *et al.* 2018). Defined in this manner, extra-economic coercion has no structural role in the system, and thus identities like race and caste cannot aspire to become focal points for left politics that seek to challenge capitalism. It is precisely here that Ambedkar's and Mariátegui's views problematize this line of reasoning by highlighting the cross pollination between social oppression and class exploitation and by situating these interactions in the larger context of the world-system. As a precursor to many influential dependency arguments, Mariátegui, as we have noted earlier, stressed how the global logic of imperialism impelled peripheral economies into a race to the bottom, in which staying ahead of the pack depended on the ability of each and every peripheral economy to utilize the most brutal, extra-economic mechanisms of wage and labour control. The social structure of these societies, moreover, was such that the native bourgeoisies, in alliance with the landlord classes, had no incentive to transform these arrangements. These extra-economic forms of coercion, in turn, were sustained and institutionalized by arbitrary apparatuses like race.

This does not mean that social oppression merely reflects the economic "needs" of the system. Both Mariátegui and Ambedkar, but especially the latter, were clear that social identities, though tightly linked to economic structures also had an independent existence of their own as they came to be imbibed, reproduced and popularized even by those sections of society that found themselves under the boots of peripheral capitalism.[9] This fact, however, did not make identities any less important to the theory and politics of class struggle. Hierarchies of race or caste served to break up the exploited classes into endogamous groupings and thus weaken the possibilities of horizontal alliances amongst them. Given their persistence in society, caste and racial differences within the working classes had to be incorporated into Marxist theory. They were not mere distractions that diverted from "pure", unadulterated class struggle; instead, mounting class struggles in the conditions that existed in the peripheries required recognizing the divisions amongst the toiling majority and placing them at the forefront of socialist theory. As Ambedkar (2015: 233) put it,

> the social order prevalent in India is a matter which a socialist must deal with . . . unless he does so he cannot achieve his revolution. . . . This is only another way of saying that, turn in any direction you like, caste is the monster that crosses your path. You cannot have political reform, you cannot have economic reform, unless you kill this monster.

This observation remains as relevant today as it did back then. If socialist movements are to harbour any hopes of gaining hegemony and finding a foothold in popular movements, they must find creative ways of incorporating the demands of social reforms and melding them with revolutionary goals.

Notes

1 This chapter draws on our previously published paper, The Political Economy of Race and Caste: Revisiting the Writings of Mariátegui and Ambedkar Which Appeared in the. *Journal of Labor and Society*, 23 (3), 399–413.
2 There are, of course, several different kinds of identity movements, including utterly regressive ones like the Hindu nationalist movement in India. In this chapter, the term identity politics refers to movements of socially oppressed sections like Dalits in India or indigenous communities in Latin America.
3 See the large literature that has emerged on the intersections between class and social identities. The close links between capitalist development and the reproduction of racism from a Marxist perspective have been investigated by Botwinick (2018), Roediger (1999), Lebowitz (2006), Singh (2016), Bhattacharyya (2018) and Robinson (2000). There is also a large literature on gender, capitalism and social reproduction (Vogel 2013; Bhattacharya 2017).
4 Mariátegui's intellectual contributions have received considerable attention from scholars over the years (Vanden 1986; Chavarría 1979). For more recent sketches of Mariátegui's life and writings, see De Castro (2020) and Gonzalez (2019).
5 It is worth noting here that the Russian Revolution had a major impact on thinkers across the Global South. Lenin's writings, in particular, were extremely influential. This was also true of Mariátegui, who, as Martin Bergel (2017) notes, was deeply influenced by the events that had unfolded in Russia.
6 The link between national liberation struggles and socialism has been contentious. The tradition of "Political Marxism" for example, has tended to polemicize against the dependency tradition for elevating struggles for national liberation over and above class struggles (Brenner 1977). Post-colonial scholarship maintains a similar hostility towards developmentalist, anti-dependency intellectual streams. In contrast, there is an important tradition that has emerged from within the Global South that has tended to view socialism, anti-imperialism and auto-centric development and closely related to one another (Sader 2011; Guevara 1967; Amin 1990). For a further discussion, see Sirohi and Bhupatiraju (2021).
7 Mariategui's discussions on religion and his attempts to combine historical materialism with idealist undertones find a sharp parallel with Ambedkar's views on religion. Part of Mariategui's disillusionment with the Western civilizational model was its uncritical celebration of reason and science, which were placed over and above spiritual and ethical values. For a discussion on Mariategui's romanticism, see Löwy (1998, 2008). For further discussions on Ambedkar's views on Buddhism, see Rao (2009), Kumar (2015) and Skaria (2015).
8 For the classical justifications for delinking, see Amin (1990, 2013) and Patnaik and Patnaik (2016). More recently, important debates have emerged from the left over the overall strategy of the left with respect to the EU (Lapavitsas 2019; Šumonja 2019).
9 Roediger (1999) develops this line of thought in the American context.

References

Alcoff, L. M. (2011). An Epistemology for the Next Revolution. *Transmodernity: Journal of Peripheral Cultural Production of the Luso-Hispanic World*, 1 (2), 67–78.
Ambedkar, B. R. (2003). Buddha and the Future of His Religion. In *Dr. Babasaheb Ambedkar, Writings and Speeches, Vol. 17 Part 2*. New Delhi: Dr. Ambedkar Foundation, Ministry of Social Justice & Empowerment, Govt. of India, 97–108.
Ambedkar, B. R. (2014a). Castes in India: Their Mechanism, Genesis and Development. In *Dr. Babasaheb Ambedkar, Writings and Speeches*, Vol. 1. New Delhi: Dr. Ambedkar Foundation, Ministry of Social Justice & Empowerment, Govt. of India, 3–22.

Ambedkar, B. R. (2014b). In the Plenary Session: Speech Delivered in the Round Table Conference (First Session). In *Dr. Babasaheb Ambedkar, Writings and Speeches*, Vol. 2. New Delhi: Dr. Ambedkar Foundation, Ministry of Social Justice & Empowerment, Govt. of India, 503–509.

Ambedkar, B. R. (2014c). The Untouchables and the Pax Britannica. In *Dr. Babasaheb Ambedkar, Writings and Speeches*, Vol. 12. New Delhi: Dr. Ambedkar Foundation, Ministry of Social Justice & Empowerment, Govt. of India, 75–147.

Ambedkar, B. R. (2015). *Annihilation of Caste*. New Delhi: Navayana.

Ambedkar, B. R. (2019). *India and Communism*. New Delhi: Leftword.

Amin, S. (1990). *Delinking: Towards a Polycentric World*. London: Zed Books.

Amin, S. (2013). *The Implosion of Contemporary Capitalism*. New York: Monthly Review Press.

Anderson, K. B. (2007). The Rediscovery and Persistence of the Dialectic in Philosophy and in World Politics. In: S. Budgen, S. Kouvelakis, and S. Žižek (Eds.), *Lenin Reloaded: Towards a Politics of Truth*. Durham and London: Duke University Press, 120–147.

Anderson, K. B. (2010). *Marx at the Margins: On Nationalism, Ethnicity, and Non-Western Societies*. Chicago: University of Chicago Press.

Angotti, T. (1986). The Contributions of José Carlos Mariátegui to Revolutionary Theory. *Latin American Perspectives*, 13 (2), 33–57.

Anievas, A. and Nisancioglu, K. (2014). The Poverty of Political Marxism. *International Socialist Review*, 94. Retrieved from: https://isreview.org/issue/94/poverty-political-marxism [Viewed 29/06/2020]

Becker, M. (2006). Mariátegui, the Comintern, and the Indigenous Question in Latin America. *Science & Society*, 70 (4), 450–479.

Bergel, M. (2017). José Carlos Mariátegui and the Russian Revolution: Global Modernity and Cosmopolitan Socialism in Latin America. *South Atlantic Quarterly*, 116 (4), 727–744.

Bhattacharya T. (Ed.) (2017). *Social Reproduction Theory: Remapping Class, Recentering Oppression*. London: Pluto Press.

Bhattacharyya, G. (2018). *Rethinking Racial Capitalism*. Lanham, MD: Rowman & Littlefield.

Botwinick, H. (2018). *Persistent Inequalities: Wage Disparity Under Capitalist Competition*. Leiden: Brill.

Brenner, R. (1977). The Origins of Capitalist Development: A Critique of Neo-Smithian Marxism. *New Left Review*, 1 (104), 25–92.

Byrd, J. A., Goldstein, A., Melamed, J. and Reddy, C. (2018). Predatory Value: Economies of Dispossession and Disturbed Relationalities. *Social Text*, 36 (2), 1–18.

Chavarría, J. (1979). *José Carlos Mariátegui and the Rise of Modern Peru, 1890–1930*. Albuquerque: University of New Mexico Press.

De Castro, J. E. (2020). *Bread and Beauty: The Cultural Politics of José Carlos Mariátegui*. Leiden and Boston: Brill.

Deshpande, A. and Darity, W. (2003). Boundaries of Clan and Color: An Introduction. In *Boundaries of Clan and Color: Transitional Comparisons of Inter-Group Disparity*. London: Routledge, 1–13.

Frankel, F. (2005). *India's Political Economy, 1947–2004: The Gradual Revolution*. New Delhi: Oxford University Press.

Fraser, N. (2000). Rethinking Recognition. *New Left Review*, 3, 107–120.

Gaikwad, S. M. (1998). Ambedkar and Indian Nationalism. *Economic and Political Weekly*, 33 (10), 515–518.

Galeano, E. (1997). *Open Veins of Latin America: Five Centuries of the Pillage of a Continent*. New York: Monthly Review Press.

Gonzalez, M. (2019). *In the Red Corner: The Marxism of José Carlos Mariátegui*. Chicago: Haymarket Books.

Goyal, Y. (2019). On Transnational Analogy: Thinking Race and Caste With W. E. B. Du Bois and Rabindranath Tagore. *Atlantic Studies*, 16 (1), 54–71.

Guevara, E. (1967). Message to the Tricontinental. In R. E. Bonachea, and N. P. Valdes (Eds.), *Che: Selected Works of Ernesto Guevara*. Cambridge, MA: MIT Press, 170–182.

Guru, G. (1998). Understanding Ambedkar's Construction of National Movement. *Economic and Political Weekly*, 33 (4), 156–157.

Guru, G. (2016). Nationalism as the Framework for Dalit Self-realization. *Brown Journal of World Affairs*, 23 (1), 239–252.

Hale, C. (1986). Political and social ideas in Latin America, 1870–1930. In L. Bethell (Ed.), *The Cambridge History of Latin America*. Cambridge: Cambridge University Press, 367–442.

Harding, N. (1983). *Lenin's Political Thought: Theory and Practice in the Democratic and Socialist Revolutions*. London and Basingstoke: Macmillan Press.

Hardt, M. and Negri, A. (2000). *Empire*. Cambridge: Harvard University Press.

Harvey, D. (2014). *Seventeen Contradictions and the End of Capitalism*. New York: Oxford University Press.

Helleiner, E. and Rosales, A. (2017). Toward Global IPE: The Overlooked Significance of the Haya-Mariátegui Debate. *International Studies Review*, 19 (4), 667–691.

Hobsbawm, E. (1996). Identity Politics and the Left. *New Left Review*, 217, 38–47.

Karat, P. (2011). The Challenge of Identity Politics. *The Marxist*, 27 (1–2), 39–50.

Kay, C. (2011). *Latin American Theories of Development and Underdevelopment*. New York: Routledge.

Kim, D. H. (2015). José Mariátegui's East-South Decolonial Experiment. *Comparative and Continental Philosophy*, 7 (2), 157–179.

Kumar, A. (2015). *Radical Equality: Ambedkar, Gandhi, and the Risk of Democracy*. Stanford: Stanford University Press.

Lapavitsas, C. (2019). *The Left Case against the EU*. London: Polity Press.

Lauesen, T. and Cope, Z. (2015). Imperialism and the Transformation of Values Into Prices. *Monthly Review*, 67 (3), 54–67.

LeBaron, G. and Gore, E. (2020). Gender and Forced Labour: Understanding the Links in Global Cocoa Supply Chains. *The Journal of Development Studies*, 56 (6), 1095–1117.

Lebowitz, M. (2006). The Politics of Assumption, the Assumption of Politics. *Historical Materialism*, 14 (2), 29–47.

Lenin, V. I. (1904 [1977]). *One Step Forward, Two Steps Back, Lenin Collected Works*, Vol. 7. Moscow: Progress Publishers.

Löwy, M. (1998). Marxism and Romanticism in the work of José Carlos Mariátegui. *Latin American Perspectives*, 25 (4), 76–88.

Löwy, M. (2008). Communism and Religion: José Carlos Mariátegui's Revolutionary Mysticism. *Latin American Perspectives*, 35 (2), 71–79.

Maddison, A. (2010). *Class Structure and Economic Growth: India and Pakistan Since the Moghuls*. New York: Routledge.

Mariátegui, J. C. (1971). *Seven Interpretative Essays on Peruvian Reality*. Austin: University of Texas Press. Retrieved from: www.marxists.org/archive/mariateg/works/7-interpretive-essays/index.htm [Viewed 11/07/2020]

Mariátegui, J. C. (2011a). The Land Problem. In H. E. Vanden, and M. Becker (Eds.), *José Carlos Mariátegui: An Anthology*. New York: Monthly Review Press, 66–109.

Mariátegui, J. C. (2011b). Anniversary and Balance Sheet. In H. E. Vanden, and M. Becker (Eds.), *José Carlos Mariátegui: An Anthology*. New York: Monthly Review Press, 118–121.

Mariátegui, J. C. (2011c). Colonial Economy. In H. E. Vanden, and M. Becker (Eds.), *José Carlos Mariátegui: An Anthology*. New York: Monthly Review Press, 122–123.

Mariátegui, J. C. (2011d). Peru's Principal Problem. In H. E. Vanden, and M. Becker (Eds.), *José Carlos Mariátegui: An Anthology*. New York: Monthly Review Press, 126–129.

Mariátegui, J. C. (2011e). Message to the Workers. In H. E. Vanden, and M. Becker (Eds.), *José Carlos Mariátegui: An Anthology*. New York: Monthly Review Press, 157–161.

Mariátegui, J. C. (2011f). Anti-Imperialist Point of View. In H. E. Vanden, and M. Becker (Eds.), *José Carlos Mariátegui: An Anthology*. New York: Monthly Review Press, 231–237.

Mariátegui, J. C. (2011g). The Problem of Race in Latin America. In H. E. Vanden, and M. Becker (Eds.), *José Carlos Mariátegui: An Anthology*. New York: Monthly Review Press, 261–279.

Mariátegui, J. C. (2011h). Man and Myth. In H. E. Vanden, and M. Becker (Eds.), *José Carlos Mariátegui: An Anthology*. New York: Monthly Review Press, 320–324.

Marx, K. and Engels, F. (2007). *Manifesto of the Communist Party*. New York: International Publishers.

Mosquera, C. C. (2018). Jose Carlos Mariategui: Welding Marxism and Indigenism in Latin America Today. *Journal of Labor and Society*, 21 (1), 5–17.

Nathan, D. and Kalpana, V. (2007). *Issues in the Analysis of Global Value Chains and Their Impact on Employment and Incomes in India* (Discussion Paper Series). Geneva: International Institute for Labour Studies, ILO.

Noakes, C. (2021). *Selected Works of Jose Carlos Mariategui*. London: Iskra Books.

Omvedt, G. (1994). *Dalits and the Democratic Revolution: Dr Ambedkar and the Dalit Movement in Colonial India*. New Delhi: Sage Publications.

Palat, R., Barr, K., Matson, J., Bahl, V. and Ahmad, N. (1986). The Incorporation and Peripheralization of South Asia, 1600–1950. *Review (Fernand Braudel Center)*, 10 (1), 171–208.

Pandey, G. (Ed.) (2010). *Subaltern Citizens and Their Histories: Investigations From India and the USA*. London: Routledge.

Pandey, G. (2013). *A History of Prejudice: Race, Caste and Difference in India and the United States*. Cambridge: Cambridge University Press.

Patnaik, U. and Patnaik, P. (2016). *A Theory of Imperialism*. New York: Columbia University Press.

Phillips, N. (2013). Unfree Labour and Adverse Incorporation in the Global Economy: Comparative Perspectives on Brazil and India. *Economy and Society*, 42 (2), 171–196.

Prashad, V. (2017). *Red Star Over the Third World*. New Delhi: LeftWord.

Quijano, A. (2000). Coloniality of Power, Eurocentrism, and Latin America. *Nepantla: Views from South*, 1 (3), 533–580.

Quijano, A. (2007). Coloniality and Modernity/Rationality. *Cultural Studies*, 21 (2–3), 168–178.

Rao, A. (2009). *The Caste Question: Dalits and the Politics of Modern India*. Berkeley and Los Angeles: University of California Press.

Reddy, D. (2005). The Ethnicity of Caste. *Anthropological Quarterly*, 78 (3), 543–584.

Reed, A. (2013). Marx, Race, and Neoliberalism. *New Labor Forum*, 22 (1), 49–57.

Reed, A. (2018). Antiracism: A Neoliberal Alternative to a Left. *Dialectical Anthropology*, 42 (2), 105–115.

Rioux, S. (2013). The Fiction of Economic Coercion: Political Marxism and the Separation of Theory and History. *Historical Materialism*, 21 (4), 92–128.

Robinson, C. (2000 [1983]). *Black Marxism: The Making of the Black Radical Tradition*. Chapel Hill: University of North Carolina Press.

Roediger, D. R. (1999). *The Wages of Whiteness: Race and the Making of the American Working Class*. London: Verso.

Roy, A. (2015). The Doctor and the Saint: An Introduction. In B. R. Ambedkar (Ed.), *Annihilation of Caste*. New Delhi: Navayana Publishing.

Roy Chowdhury, A. (2020). An 'Un-imagined Community': The Entangled Genealogy of an Exclusivist Nationalism in Myanmar and the Rohingya Refugee Crisis. *Social Identities*, 26 (5), 590–607.

Roy Chowdhury, A. and Abid, A. (2022). Treading the Border of (il)legality: Statelessness, "Amphibian Life," and the Rohingya "Boat People" of Asia. *Inter-Asia Cultural Studies*, 23 (1), 68–85.

Sader, E. (2011). *The New Mole: Paths of the Latin American Left*. London: Verso.

Seth, S. (1989). Marxism and the Question of Nationalism in a Colonial Context: The Case of British India. PhD Thesis, Australian National University.

Singh, N. P. (2016). On Race, Violence, and So-Called Primitive Accumulation. *Social Text*, 34 (3), 27–50.

Sirohi, R. A. (2019). *From Developmentalism to Neoliberalism: A Comparative Analysis of Brazil and India*. Singapore: Palgrave Macmillan.

Sirohi, R. A. and Bhupatiraju, S. (2021). *Reassessing the Pink Tide: Lessons From Brazil and Venezuela*. Singapore: Palgrave Macmillan.

Skaria, A. (2015). Ambedkar, Marx and the Buddhist Question, *South Asia: Journal of South Asian Studies*, 38 (3), 450–465.

Slate, N. (2012). *Colored Cosmopolitanism: The Shared Struggle for Freedom in the United States and India*. Cambridge, MA: Harvard University Press.

Smith, J. (2016). *Imperialism in the 21st Century*. New York: Monthly Review Press.

Šumonja, M. (2019). The Habermas-Streeck Debate Revisited: Syriza and the Illusions of the Left-Europeanism. *Capital & Class*, 43 (3), 437–458.

Teltumbde, A. (2018). *Republic of Caste: Thinking Equality in the Time of Neoliberal Hindutva*. New Delhi: Navayana.

Teltumbde, A. (2019). Introduction. In B. R. Ambedkar (Ed.), *India and Communism*. New Delhi: Leftword.

Vanden, H. (1986). *National Marxism in Latin America: José Carlos Mariátegui's Thought and Praxis*. Boulder: Lynne Rienner Publishers.

Vogel, L. (2013). *Marxism and the Oppression of Women: Toward a Unitary Theory*. Leiden: Brill.

Wade, P. (2010). *Race and Ethnicity in Latin America*. 2nd edition. London: Pluto press.

Webber, J. R. (2015). The Indigenous Community as "Living Organism": José Carlos Mariátegui, Romantic Marxism, and Extractive Capitalism in the Andes. *Theory and Society*, 44 (6), 575–598.

Wood, E. M. (2000). *Democracy against Capitalism: Renewing Historical Materialism*. Cambridge: Cambridge University Press.

Yountae, A. (2017). Secularism Meets Coloniality: Mariategui's Andean Political Theology. *Political Theology*, 18 (8), 677–692.

3   Memories of Underdevelopment
Miguel Ángel Asturias's Chronicles on India

In a poem titled "Problems of Underdevelopment" ("Problemas del sub-desarrollo") written in the 1970s, the Afro-Cuban poet Nicolás Guillén (1902–1989) pointed to the coloniality of knowledge that excluded Latin America from world history and to the skewed criteria that decide what constitutes knowledge at all. Guillén (1973: n.p.) wrote:

> Monsieur Dupont calls you uncultured
> because you cannot tell who was
> Victor Hugo's favourite grandson.
> Herr Müller has started to scream
> because you do not know (exactly)
> the day that Bismarck died.
> Your friend Mr. Smith
> an Englishman or Yankee, I cannot tell,
> becomes incensed when you write Shell.
> (It seems you leave out an "l"
> and, what's more, you pronounce it *chel*.)
> Okay, and what of it?
> When it's your turn,
> make them say cacarajícara
> and ask them where is the Aconcagua
> and who was Sucré
> and just where on this planet
> did Martí die.
> And please:
> tell them to always speak to you in Spanish.[1]

The very title of this remarkable poem calls attention to a key concept elaborated by the Latin American economists of the Dependency School in the 1970s: that underdevelopment in the Third World was a consequence of its historical relations with the developed world and not an "original" state from which it could aspire to catch up with the developed capitalist world. The

DOI: 10.4324/9781003316084-4

global inequality between the North and the South, anti-imperialist scholars argued, was sustained not only by political, military and economic means but also through cultural ones. In fact, thinkers like Celso Furtado came to think of the

> phenomenon of dependency, except the features that had developed during the period of colonial domination . . . in cultural terms through the transplantation of consumption patterns . . . that projected dependency in technological terms, inscribing it into the productive structure.
>
> (Cunha and Britto 2017: 16)

The poem raises precisely these concerns and, moreover, turns the reader's attention to "the necessary connection between politics, economics, and culture" (Harlow 1987: 32), urging us to question the legitimacy of such knowledge, which leaves out local histories and the languages and cultures of the peripheral nations as inconsequential while privileging even the most insignificant trivia of Euro-American cultures. In fact, throughout the 20th century, intellectuals from both India and Latin America actively sought out new points of cultural reference beyond the hegemonic domination of the powerful North over knowledge production that the poem refers to. The imaginary of a Global South has potentiated the search and recovery of such pathways of intellectual encounters beyond the binary of the metropole and colony and has, in fact, placed them at the very core of the articulation of the new imaginary. As recent as the term may be, in as much as it reflects the geopolitical shifts of our times and the attendant aspirations for pluriversality emanating from the erstwhile colonially subjugated peoples, it has historical continuity.

In this chapter, we look at one such intellectual encounter that has remained surprisingly occluded: the participation of Latin American Nobel Laureate Miguel Ángel Asturias (Guatemala, 1899–1974) in the Asian Writers Conference (AWC) held in New Delhi in December 1956. Miguel Ángel Asturias, one of Latin America's foremost writers of the 20th century, is considered a forerunner, along with the Venezuelan Arturo Uslar Pietri and the Cuban Alejo Carpentier, of the new Latin American novel that would translate into the "Boom" in the 1960s. His novel *El Señor Presidente* (*The President*, 1946) is considered the first work of the Boom. Written in the 1920s, though published much later, the novel uses a surrealism deeply imbued with Maya-Kiché consciousness to take the reader through the nightmare of Manuel Estrada Cabrera's dictatorship (1898–1920). This feature, a constant in his later fiction too, is always accompanied by a scathing critique of international capital and its devastating effects on the Guatemalan peasantry. Asturias was awarded the Lenin Peace Prize in 1966 and, in 1967, the Nobel for literature.

The AWC, which the Guatemalan writer attended, was a landmark event in the cultural consolidation of the idea of the Third World and a precursor to the more widely discussed First Afro-Asian Writers Conference that would take place two years later in Tashkent, Soviet Central Asia, in October 1958. The conference responded to the growing aspirations for intellectual autonomy in the Third World. As waves of national liberation struggles swept across Asia, Africa and Latin America, transnational solidarity became the hallmark of cultural and literary production. After this conference, Asturias wrote several "chronicles"[2] on India, which are anthologized in the book *Viajes, Ensayos y Fantasías* (1981) [Travels, Essays and Fantasies], a collection of mainly newspaper articles by the Nobel laureate compiled by Richard Callan. Asturias also translated into Spanish, in collaboration with his wife Blanca Mora de Araujo, the famous novel of Bhabani Bhattacharya, *He Who Rides the Tiger* (1954). The history of these "pre-postcolonial" Third-Worldist internationalisms needs to be reconstructed (Halim 2019b). It is only recently that Global South studies examining the South-South connected cultural histories have begun looking at the Third Worldist anti-colonial networks of writers and artists that came up in the 1950s and 1960s of the last century. These studies have brought into focus collaborations across Africa and Asia (Halim 2012, 2019a; Han 2018; Jansen 2019; Yoon 2012, 2015, 2018). The AWC, hitherto completely forgotten, has recently also been the object of some studies in the framework of Global South studies, though mainly in the context of India-China literary relations and the complex cultural politics of the Cold War that animated them (Jia 2019, 2021; Mangalagiri 2021). The AWC was an incipient effort at the inaugural moment of the post-Bandung transnational flow of intellectual thought that later evolved into a larger platform of writers, artists and intellectuals from the newly liberated countries of Asia and Africa. It is therefore an important part of the cultural legacy of Bandung. Miguel Ángel Asturias's chronicles on India and the translation of Bhabani Bhattacharya's novel into Spanish, which he did in collaboration with Blanca Mora de Araujo, embody "the Bandung spirit" and serve as a concrete instantiation of decolonial experimentation, which was the hallmark of the Third Worldist cultural project initiated after Bandung. This cultural project was marked by Afro-Asian solidarity and an anti-colonial internationalism in which the cementing of cultural relations was seen as a means of creating an alternative to the reigning western aesthetic supremacy. The Final Communiqué of the Asian-African Conference laid special stress on renewing and strengthening cultural contact amongst African and Asian peoples, as well as with other cultures, as a means of promoting world peace and understanding (Asia-Africa 1955). Miguel Ángel Asturias's chronicles on India exemplify the manner in which many Latin American writers would approach India in their writings all through the 20th century – a turn from writing of it as "Orient", the Other, to seeing it as the "Third World", of which they themselves were a part. In doing so, these chronicles represent an important body of writing that brings Latin America into the ambit of literary solidarity that was being constituted across the Afro-Asian networks and exemplifies the synergy of intellectual thought in the framework of South-South exchange that has been present in the intellectual encounters between India and Latin America.

Latin America's Epistemic Engagement With India

Ever since the colossal equivocation of Christopher Columbus, who, believing that he had reached India, called the men and women inhabiting those newly discovered lands Indians, the appellation as well as the subsequent shared history of colonization turned India and Latin America into Europe's "others", not only reflecting on each other through a mediated gaze but also subverting that very gaze. A noteworthy perspective coming from the Argentine-Mexican philosopher Enrique Dussel privileges pre-Columbian connections between Asia and America. Arguing for a non-Eurocentric vision of history, he states that contrary to the usual college and university history programmes that first mention them in 1492, Amerindians had history prior to the so-called discovery of America. Dussel posits the Pacific as an important contact zone and places the Amerindians in an Asian context, demonstrating that they inhabited the extreme east of the Orient and were "Asiatic in race, language, and religion" (Dussel 1997: 84). Such a shift from a trans-Atlantic to a trans-Pacific perspective unhinges Latin America and Asia from their identitarian relationship with the West and orients Pre-Columbian America towards the East and vice versa.

Studies on the global history of early modernity have also highlighted the web of interconnectedness between the Americas and Asia during the colonial era through a thriving trans-Pacific trade (Uchmany 2003). The Manila Galleon as a system of trade lasted two and a half centuries from 1565 until 1815, connecting South Asia, South East Asia and East Asia with New Spain through Portuguese and Spanish colonial regulatory controls in *Estado da Índia* and the Philippines, respectively. The introduction of Asian merchandise in exchange, for example, of silver via the Pacific, not only opened an alternative to the Atlantic trade in the Americas but also stimulated a certain aesthetic of consumption in the local elites such that "these *social objects* . . . left a footprint in the cultural formation of these societies" (Villamar 2021: 147). Octavio Paz, in his celebrated essay *Vislumbres de la India* (*In Light of India*, 1995), mentions the legend of the *China poblana*, the Indian princess "Mirra", who landed in Mexico in the 17th century, sailing in one of the ships of the Manila Galleon, and became the venerated Catarina de San Juan. The *China poblana* is a powerful example of the cultural synthesis that the trans-Pacific movement of commodities and people produced in the realm of popular culture.

Their gradual Hispanization during colonial rule veered the Americas definitively into the orbit of the West, and for the majority of the creole elite, the debate after independence as to what models the new republics ought to fashion themselves on was solely about choosing between Old World civilizational values and the materialist utilitarianism of the emerging powerful neighbour of the North. Interestingly, there was a subterranean Orientalism that, as in the case of Argentina, conceived of the internal "Other", meaning the native Indian and "uncultured" mestizo, as the barbaric Oriental. Such comparisons abound in the foundational text of Argentinean nationhood, *Facundo* (Bergel 2015; Civantos 2005), but were equally prevalent, for example, even in the cultural discourse of post-independence Mexico, where the intellectual elite had forged the idea of Mexican-ness, valorizing its civilizational antiquity and including the native Indian in the construction of the idea of a modern Mexican nation. In an insightful essay on Orientalist discourse in post-colonial Mexico, Nancy Vogeley (1995) has shown that the universal popularity of the cultural *topoi* of "civilization" and "barbarism" in postcolonial Mexico can be ascribed to the influence of 19th-century European Orientalist discourse, which was arriving through the Italian Opera and newspapers and provided the newly independent nation with definitions of the European Self and the Oriental Other in contexts other than its own experience of colonial othering. The 19th-century colonization of Asia and the knowledge produced subsequently in these regions also started reaching Latin America through various channels and greatly influenced its perception of the Orient, which had now replaced the Americas as a discursive space in the European colonial imagination.

By the end of the 19th century, Latin America had been thoroughly incorporated into the orbit of capitalist modernization. The 1890s saw a debilitated Spain lose its last colonies, and North American expansionism was at work with the annexation of Puerto Rico and intervention in Cuba in 1898. Such a historical conjuncture made Latin American intellectuals seek distance from European colonialism as well as from North American instrumental reason, with an awareness of the emergence of a new kind of expansionist interventionism. Lenin noted that it was with the Spanish-American War (1898) and the Anglo-Boer War (1899–1902) that "the economic and also the political literature of the two hemispheres has more and more often adopted the term 'imperialism' in order to describe the present era" (Lenin 1974: 195). The intellectual and artistic awakening that informed Latin American modernist poetry sought to do away with colonial cultural models and attempted to create a distinct idiom of self-representation. Iris Zavala, therefore, considers Latin American modernism to be an anti-imperialist "narrative of liberation" (1992:5), which gave rise to "a new decolonized modern subject" (1992: 8) and created "a 'third world,' which was . . . an open possibility . . . neither European nor North American" (1992: 2). Thus Gupta (2019: 6) suggests that "Latin American *modernismo*'s interest in the Orient or its cosmopolitanism is not just a stylistic device, but linked to significant questions of identity formation", given that *modernistas* like José Martí, Rubén Darío, Gutiérrez Nájera, Julián del Casal or Leopoldo Lugones, amongst others, were forging a new poetic idiom that would replace the stylistic codes of the metropolis. The orientalism of the *modernistas* should be seen in the context of their rejection of the materialist utilitarianism and expansionist appetites of their northern neighbour, in addition to seeking "new social relations away from the asphyxiating local" and to "connect alterities outside the colonial (and local) systems of relation" (Zavala 1992: 49).

By the early 20th century, the questioning of European superiority became even more pronounced as the First World War led Latin American intellectuals to look for alternative self-definitions. Martin Bergel has assiduously pointed out in his brilliant and nuanced study on Argentine intellectual thought, which is in fact applicable to Latin America in general, that by the 1920s, in the measure that Europe was being displaced as the cultural centre, there came about an inversion of Orientalism in Latin American intellectual thought, giving rise to a proto-Third Worldism that developed along two fundamental axes: anti-imperialism and spiritualism (Bergel 2015: 15). India's colonial situation and the struggle against British imperialism were not alien to Latin American thinkers and writers who empathized with India's struggle given their own colonial past and their own relation to subjugation in the world capitalist order. The 1920s were also times of the emergence of indigenous socialist thought in Latin America. As noted in earlier chapters, José Carlos Mariátegui's book, *Seven Interpretive Essays on Peruvian Reality*, is a masterpiece of Latin American indigenism, but what is less known is that Mariátegui is also the author of some incisive essays on India's freedom struggle. These essays from 1925 to 1930 go beyond the towering figures of Gandhi and Tagore and cover a sharp analysis of the various facets, ideological underpinnings and movements that made up those turbulent years. In an important chronicle published in a Peruvian journal in January 1930, just a few months before his death, Mariátegui covers the Simon Commission and the martyrdom of Lala Lajpat Rai in 1928, as well as an analysis of the various currents and tendencies within the Indian National Congress.[3] Additionally, several Latin American thinkers were attracted to the alternative that the Orient offered them, displacing Europe, which was seen as having lost its spiritual values. Indian intellectual traditions figure prominently in this process. There is a vast corpus of texts in which Indian philosophy, its literature and intellectual thought are seen as resources for Latin American rejuvenation. One can cite several examples: Mexico's literacy campaigns in the 1920s were spurred by the Education Minister José Vasconcelos's vision of amalgamating Mexican traditions with yoga and vegetarianism, showing the instrumentalization of "Indian 'spiritual' practices within the State imperatives of development and modernization" (Torres-Rodriguez 2015: 89); translations of various Indian texts by influential men of letters, for example, the songs of Kabir in Argentina in 1915–1916 by enlightened statesmen and heterodox intellectuals such as Joaquin V. Gonzalez and Carlos Muzzio Saenz Peña based on Tagore's versions (Gupta 2019); the reception of theosophical currents across the continent and their enormous influence not only on intellectuals such as Vasconcelos, as mentioned earlier, but also on Nobel Laureate Gabriela Mistral from

Chile, Haya de la Torre from Peru, César Augusto Sandino from Nicaragua and many others in visualizing an anti-imperialist, indigenist social project (Devés Valdés and Melgar Bao 2007); all of these show a definite engagement with India in the Latin Americanist ideology of this period.

In India, in the writings of figures like Tagore, Nehru and M.N. Roy, one also finds a persistent search for new intellectual horizons for the emerging nation beyond the western enclosures. Roy's journey from an Indian freedom fighter to founder of the Mexican Communist Party is a paradigmatic example of the trajectory taken by several intellectuals and activists of that time (Goebel 2014; Alonso 2017). Tagore's extensive travels to East Asia and Latin America and the writings that these voyages produced reflect a powerful yearning for a "different universalism" to counter the European monopoly over cosmopolitan claims (Bose and Pande 2011). Thus, Gupta (2019: 6) notes that "Tagore's modernist position for the nation coming into being finds a parallel in the conception of America in the turn of the century Latin American *modernistas* and their decolonializing impulse". Seen in this manner, José Martí's famous essay "Nuestra América" (Our America, 1891), for example "was a concrete ideological interpellation connoting a decolonized and self-determined 'birth of a nation'" (Zavala 1992: 37). Martí's turn of the century essay, considered a foundational text of Latin American identity discourse, posits the political construct of "Our America" as against the Pan-American project of Washington's inter-American policy of continental solidarity, in which the United States would have the leading role.

The stirrings of a potent South-South dialogue through anti-imperialist internationalist networks have therefore been present since the beginning of the 20th century in the epistemic engagement between India and Latin America, and the emergence of an Independent Indian state after the dismantling of the British empire, the moment that interests us in this chapter, would further consolidate these potentialities.

Asian Writers' Conference, the Bandung Spirit and Miguel Ángel Asturias

By the 1950s, liberation movements in Asia and Africa, having given birth to newly independent nations that had fought against European colonial powers, had succeeded in redrawing three-fourths of the world map. The Bandung Conference (April 18–24, 1955), which brought together 29 of these newly liberated developing nations on a joint political platform, was primarily an Asian-African initiative, and Latin America would become part of a joint anti-imperialist platform with Asia and Africa only later, with the Tricontinental Conference in Havana in 1966 and the formation of the Organization for the Solidarity with the Peoples of Asia, Africa and Latin America (OSPAAAL).[4] This could be one of the reasons why the Guatemalan Nobel Laureate's participation in the AWC and this important body of texts by him on India have remained underserved. Though all of Latin America, with the exception of Cuba and Puerto Rico, had gained independence at the beginning of the 19th century, the region had been neo-colonized by the United States, which, in the famous words of liberator Simón Bolívar in 1829 itself, appeared "destined by Providence to plague the Americas with misery in the name of freedom" (Bolívar *et al.* 2003: 173). US intervention in Cuba in the 1898 Spanish American War was a clear example of its expansionist appetite, which only grew with time to match that of the erstwhile and now waning European empires. The creation of instruments such as the Organization of American States in 1948 in the name of Pan-Americanism consolidated US hegemony in the region, placing Latin America firmly in its area of influence during the entire Cold War period. It is in this context that the visit of Miguel Ángel Asturias to India in 1956 to participate in the Asian Writers' Conference acquires immense importance, as Latin America had not been directly a part of the Bandung process. However, while the triumph of the Cuban revolution in 1959 brought Latin America into the fold of anti-colonial resistance platforms of the 1950s and 1960s along with Asia and Africa (Young 2005: 15–16), Latin American anti-imperialist sectors had already been combating the expansionist neo-colonialism of the powerful neighbour of the north. Just a year prior to the Bandung meeting, Miguel Ángel Asturias's homeland, Guatemala, had witnessed a CIA-backed bloody coup against the elected government of Jacobo Árbenz. The moderately liberal Árbenz government expropriated some 1.4 million acres of arable land, including huge properties of the US company United Fruit in Guatemala, as part of its agrarian reform, which is calculated to have benefitted five hundred thousand Guatemalans (Gleijeses 1991: 149–170). At the X Inter-American Conference convened in March 1954 in Caracas, US Secretary of State John Foster Dulles mobilized the delegates against the Árbenz government, alleging that it represented a communist threat to the Americas. As a delegate to the Conference, Miguel Ángel Asturias, representing the Árbenz government as Ambassador of Guatemala to El Salvador since October 1953, had defended the Arbenz government. A few months later, in June 1954, the CIA engineered the overthrow of the Arbenz government through armed mercenaries, and Asturias was not only recalled as ambassador, but he was also stripped of his nationality. Asturias was forced into exile in Argentina (Bellini 1999: 207), and his travel to India happened under a special Argentine passport. Thus, Miguel Ángel Asturias's journey to India happened at a point in time when he was politically in his most active and mature phase. Though Asturias had never espoused political militancy, his liberal outlook led him to recognize the socio-economic injustices of his time. It was also in the decade of the 1950s when Miguel Ángel Asturias wrote his famous "Banana trilogy"[5] marked by the magical realist narrative technique that he had already developed in his most enduring work, *El Señor Presidente*.

The 1955 meeting at Bandung was a political movement, but the spirit that this meeting and other similar initiatives embodied led to the establishment of a wide network of cultural and literary events and collaborations between Third World intellectuals. The Asian Writers' Conference, for the first time in modern history, brought together writers and intellectuals from 14 Asian countries (along with observers from many non-Asian countries) in an intense exchange of ideas in sessions spread over a week. The call for this conference was given at the Asian Conference for the Relaxation of International Tensions (CRIT) that was held in Delhi between April 6 and 10, 1955, just a few days before the Bandung Meet (Jansen 2019: 197).[6] Well-known Indian intellectual and novelist Dr. Mulk Raj Anand was the convenor of the conference, and in the preparatory committee meetings held in July 1956,[7] it was suggested that the aims of the conference ought to be, amongst others, to familiarize each other with the literary and cultural heritage of the Asian nations, "to inaugurate an atmosphere of tolerance and friendship in which new creative works can be provided and shared among various nations", and further the cause of the "common search for a new life in Asia" (Desai 243). The AWC provided a platform for nearly 200 writers from Asian countries to reflect on the specific context of the current literary practices in their countries, conceptualize Asian cultural unity and forge an anti-colonial poetics.[8] The conference also brought into focus the linguistic pluralism of Asia and the challenges of reading Asian literature in a multilingual environment, in which translation was envisaged as a mode of forging an Asian literary canon.

Asturias's chronicles build on many of these themes that were discussed in the AWC. He chooses the literary form of the chronicle to record his reflections and observations on questions of language, gender, caste, and class in Indian society, as well as his assessment of diverse aspects of the newly formed republic. Asturias's visit to India and his participation in the Asian Writers' Conference in December 1956 happened on his return from China, where he, accompanied by his wife Blanca Mora y Araujo, had travelled on invitation to attend the commemoration of the 20th death anniversary of poet Lu Xun, which was on October 19, 1956. After a three-month long stay in China, the couple came to New Delhi (Bellini 1999: 208)[9] to attend the AWC beginning on December 23, 1956, and stayed on for a long sojourn, visiting other cities and places. Considering that they were published in a newspaper (*El Nacional* of Caracas), Asturias's chronicles carry the intent of disseminating knowledge on post-independence India (and Asia in general) through his column on aspects that he felt needed elucidation for Latin American readers. In a chronicle titled "Los escritores de Asia y la crisis de la cultura" [Asian Writers and the Crisis of Culture] (Asturias 1981: 156–158), published on July 2, 1957, Asturias picks up the discussion around an important theme that was taken up in the AWC, that of the putative crisis of world culture. Referring to post-war despair in literary movements such as existentialism, Asturias argues that the prophets of doom, including some from India, are heralding a total collapse of human culture, but that many other writers, particularly the

Figure 3.1 Miguel Ángel Asturias (left) attending the Asian Writers' Conference in New
Delhi, December 1956. Seen in the photograph are also, the Colombian poet
Jorge Zalamea (centre), and the Romanian writer Zaharia Stancu (right).

Source: Personal collection of Miguel Ángel Asturias Amado, son of Miguel Ángel Asturias.

younger ones, believe that the crisis of western culture cannot be equated to a universal crisis. Doing so would mean disregarding what is happening in Asia:

> ¿Cómo hablar de crisis cuando nuevas savias, arrancadas de terrenos abonados por milenios de sabiduría, suben por las raíces de estos pueblos y enriquecen sus manifestaciones artísticas poco conocidas, si se quiere, pero no por eso inexistentes? . . . La fórmula tabú de "Fait à París" o "Made in England" sí está en crisis, pero no las grandes voces de poetas y escritores, novelistas, ensayistas, que enriquecen a diario en cien lenguas diferentes, el aporte de Asia a la literatura universal.

(Asturias 1981: 157)

[How can we speak of crisis when a new vital sap springing forth from a soil fertilized by millennia of wisdom, moves up through the roots of these peoples and enriches their artistic manifestations, which are perhaps not so known, but are not, for that reason, inexistent? . . . The taboo formula of "Fait à Paris" or "Made in England" is in crisis, but not the great voices of poets and writers, novelists, essayists, who daily enrich in a hundred different languages, the contribution of Asia to world literature.][10]

Asturias is clearly arguing for uncovering artistic manifestations from Asia that were operating outside the reigning canons of 20th-century literature. Questioning a conception of world literature that fails to take into account the vernacular textual cultures of the peripheries, Asturias asks his Latin American readers:

> ¿Sabemos algo nosotros de la literatura cingalesa, de los avances de la literatura bengalí, de la literatura punjabi, de la literatura urdu, de la literatura marathi? En todas estas zonas asiáticas surgen a diario obras en verso y en prosa que lejos de ser el final de una época, son el renacer de un tiempo nuevo, el empezar de un Continente que había estado postergado, el reencuentro del asiático con su personalidad, porque los pueblos se extraviaban, se sumergen en interminable épocas de duro sueño, bajo diversos dominios pero luego renacen, afloran y sobresalen, como ahora pasa en ese mundo que se quiere pretender que se siga ignorando, el mundo asiático.

[Asturias 1981: 157]

[Do we know anything about Sri Lankan literature, the advances in Bengali literature, Punjabi literature, Urdu literature, Marathi literature? In all these Asian regions, works in verse and prose appear daily, which far from being the end of an era, are the rebirth of a new epoch, the commencement of a deferred continent, the reencounter of Asia with its personality, because nations go astray, sink in endless times of deep slumber under various dominions, but they are reborn, they flourish and excel, as is happening now in this world that would still want Asia to be ignored.]

In fact, Asturias is echoing here one of the recurring themes in the interventions made by delegates of the AWC, that of an Asian resurgence: Saeed Nafsi of the Iranian delegation talked of a "renaissance of Asian cultures"; Han Sul Ya of the Korean delegation celebrated an "emergent Asia" whose people are "fully capable of thinking independently"; the delegation of North Vietnam mentioned "an awakening of Asian consciousness"; and Faiz Ahmed Faiz, as leader of the Pakistani delegation, envisaged a "cultural unity of Asian people through the unity of writers".[11] In the chronicle titled "Las lenguas en Asia" [Languages in Asia], Asturias starts by underlining how the Asian resurgence has given a new lease of life to vernacular cultures. The rest of the chronicle is a poetic tribute to the languages of India, with their varied sounds and intonations. Asturias's approach to India's linguistic pluralism is refreshingly different from the colonial technologies of knowledge-making that saw Indian multilingualism as "symptomatic of its fundamentally inchoate reality" (Kothari 2018: 9). On the contrary, Asturias, coming from a region marked by a rich though conflictive linguistic diversity, seeks parallels between the syntax of Indian languages and dialects and that of American indigenous languages. Highlighting the "abracadabrance" of sounds that he hears in the markets of Old Delhi, in Calcutta, or when descending the steps into the Ganges in Benares, Asturias sees India's tower of Babel not as divine punishment but as "un alimento saboreable de lo espiritual" [a tasteful nourishment of the spiritual] (Asturias 1981: 132).

Many of the chronicles that Asturias published on India can be read as a tourist's musings. Asturias and Blanca Mora travelled to Jaipur, Agra and also Varanasi on the recommendation of and in the company of Jorge Zalamea, the exiled Colombian writer who was in India those days as the Secretary General of the World Peace Council.[12] However, shunning the gaze of the *flâneur* in Paris as well as the exoticism of a tourist's idiom, Asturias writes as an involved participant, as someone who has a stake in the country he is visiting. His travel writing is marked by its Third Worldist approach, which can even be defined as firmly anti-orientalist. In "Ciudades para el futuro" [Cities for Future] (Asturias 1981: 164–166), Asturias expresses his marvel at Delhi, a modern city with wide roads and green spaces, a city for the future, which he says uses the concept of space from its age-old tradition. It is not a city for those "lovers of the pintoresque", who refuse to see a new life on a continent that is awakening. Of such tourists, Asturias laments that they

ven y admiran . . . los monumentos, se afanan por develar misterios que no existen sino en la fantasía dulce de los creyentes, buscan las drogas de prolongar la vida, de mejorar el placer y se erizan de espanto ante los reptiles amaestrados que bailan al son que les toca un esqueleto humano vestido con trapos blancos.

(Asturias 1981: 165)

[come and admire . . . the monuments, they strive to unveil mysteries that do not exist except in the sweet fantasy of believers, they seek drugs to prolong life, to enhance pleasure, and bristle with terror at the trained reptiles that dance to the tune being played by a human skeleton dressed in white rags.]

Instead, Asturias argues for a new type of tourist, one who, without being a prisoner of prejudice, would be able to make an objective assessment of these "Ninevehs of the future" (Asturias 1981: 166). In another chronicle titled "Desencuentros cronológicos" [Discords of Time] (Asturias 1981: 158–160), Asturias, in fact, rues that the tourist lives only in the past, visiting monuments, museums and monasteries. In order to avoid living in a romanticized past of India, he prefers to throw off the tourist from within him and escape this chronological discord. Asturias writes that only by living a normal life could he discuss with his Indian poet friends their present and their tasks for the future.

In the chronicle published on May 15, 1957, titled "Los maharadjas y las *Mil y una noches*" [The Maharajas and the *Thousand and One Nights*] (Asturias 1981: 140–142), a trip to Amber Fort near Jaipur becomes a moment not only to explain the existence of 500-odd principalities in India and the opulence of the maharajas and their life styles but also to emphasize that in the new republic, their privileges had been annulled with the expropriation and nationalization of their dominions. The maharajas and their fantastic luxuries, Asturias asserts, are a thing of the past: "El libro de las *Mil y una noches* se va cerrando en Oriente" [the book of *Thousand and One Nights* is now closing in the Orient] (Asturias 1981: 142). It is not that Asturias is blind to the complex interplay of caste, class and gender that characterizes social formations in India. But his approach is not one of condescension. The chronicle on caste, titled "La invisible prisión de las castas" [The Invisible Prison of Castes] (Asturias 1981: 151–153) is an example: Asturias begins by saying how his Latin American mind is not able to process certain phenomena, like that of royalty, for example and he wonders how some Frenchmen could believe that it was the royals who had for 20 centuries made France great. He encounters a similar perplexity, he says, with caste in India, which he sees as an invisible prison limiting the potentialities of individuals. By placing his incomprehension of the two institutions, monarchy in Europe and the caste system in India, on an equal footing, Asturias introduces a perspective that refuses to valorize one culture at the cost of another and negates any possible eurocentrism in making a case for the absurdity of caste as an institution.

In some chronicles, Asturias focuses on themes of tourist interest and curiosities like the monkeys in the temples, the astrologers, the fakirs and the saints and their omnipresence all over India, be it in Bombay, Benares or Calcutta, as well as the exasperating experiences with Asian bureaucracy, which finds its quintessential horror in India. However, the dominant tone, especially in some of the later chronicles, is that of a new resurgent India, which, like the rest of decolonized Asia, is on the path of technological modernization and cultural reawakening, albeit facing major challenges in the struggle to become a modern nation state. In the article titled "La técnica sustituye a la magia" [Technology substitutes Magic] (Asturias 1981: 163–164), Asturias calls science and technology the new religion and clearly sees the incipient developmentalist project of India as an example of how the once colonized people of Asia are using modern industries, science and technology for emancipatory ends. This was not an endorsement of crude modernist stagism of the kinds that had become popular in Western modernization theories. Rather, it stemmed from the reality that the Third World, with its history of colonialism and abject economic underdevelopment, could not possibly hope to emancipate itself from the yoke of the West unless it developed the economic wherewithal to stand on its own two feet. It was not just Asturias, of course, who saw in Third World developmentalism a certain emancipatory quality, even thinkers as far apart as Che Guevara, M.N. Roy and Jawaharlal Nehru held similar views. Che, as is well known, was an advocate of planned industrialization, but even the cosmopolitanist M.N. Roy held great value to state-led industrialization. They saw industrialization not only as a necessary step to address the immediate need of providing employment to scores of people stuck in low-paying, unproductive sectors but also as the most effective bulwark against Western domination. As Nehru put it,

> One thing is clear to me: that if we do not develop heavy industry here, then we either eliminate all modern things such as railways, airplanes and guns, as these things cannot be manufactured in small-scale industry, or else import them. But to import them from abroad is to be the slaves of foreign countries. Whenever these countries wished they could stop sending these things, bringing our work to a halt; we would thus remain slaves.
>
> (cited in Panagariya 2008: 25)

Colonial historicism had always held non-European societies as incapable of political and economic modernity, but Asturias was part of an entire generation of thinkers who rejected this and countered the prevalent idea of Asian stasis as well.

Translating for Transnational Solidarity

Miguel Ángel Asturias and Blanca Mora met several poets, writers and dignitaries during their stay in India. In her memoirs, Blanca Mora recalls having met Rajendra Prasad, President of India, as well as Jawaharlal Nehru, the Prime Minister, along with his daughter Indira Gandhi (Mora y Araujo 2017: 279–290). One of the Indian writers they met during the AWC was Bhabani Bhattacharya, whom Blanca Mora remembers as being considered one of the foremost writers of his time in India (Mora y Araujo 2017: 281). Miguel Ángel Asturias and Blanca Mora later translated his 1954 novel *He Who Rides the Tiger* into Spanish. The translation bearing the title *El que cabalga un tigre* was published in Buenos Aires in 1958. Miguel Ángel Asturias is known for his rendering into Spanish of sacred Mayan texts such as the *Popol Vuh* and the *Annals of the Cakchiqueles* in the 1920s as a young student of anthropology at the Sorbonne. These translations were a product of his commitment to the historical struggle of the indigenous people of his country, which prompted him to "recover the Maya Quiché heritage and cultural identity for world literature" (Washbourne 2011: 14). His translation of Bhabani Bhattacharya's novel into Spanish along with Blanca Mora y Araujo soon after their participation in the AWC should also be seen as part of Asturias's commitment to the project of creating a common literary canon for the Third World.

Translation, in fact, was a major theme of discussion in the AWC. The participating delegations were aware of the fact that colonialism had disrupted bonds of friendship and networks of cultural interchange amongst Asians. The translation of literary works across languages was seen as an urgent imperative. Han Sul Ya, the leader of the North Korean delegation, in his report, while emphasizing translating and introducing works of art reciprocally, exhorted all those attending the Conference that "every delegate present here, when he returns to his country, should do his best to see that the literature of other countries is translated and introduced to meet the desire and demand of the people" (Ya 1956: 24). For Sul Ya, translations of literary works were to be "weapons which play a cardinal role in mutual understanding, emotional education and in promoting solidarity" (Ya 1956: 24). Emi Siao, a well-known Chinese writer and translator, member of the Chinese delegation to the AWC and a good friend of the Asturias couple, in his intervention during the Conference highlighted the enormous translation work China had carried out: some 2,342,320 volumes of translated works from many Asian countries such as India, Japan, Burma, Mongolia, Korea, Vietnam, Turkey, Indonesia and Iran. Many of the writers participating in the AWC were surely well aware of how translation was also playing a central role in forging a transnational socialist identity. For example, from the 1930s itself, the Soviet Publishing House of Literature in Foreign Languages (that would later become Progress Publishers) had an impressive array of publications in West European languages, and in the very first decade after the Second World War, it was also publishing in Afro-Arabic and Indian languages (Djagalov 2019: 78). This ambitious translational activity had succeeded in reinventing the canon of world literature in the Third World countries where these translations were read avidly. As Vijay Prashad puts it succinctly "Generations in the Global South grew up with Soviet books on our shelves" (Prashad 2019: 13). Lydia Liu also mentions the case of the Chinese journal *Yiwen* [Translations], which was renamed *Shijie wenxue* [World Literature] in January 1959 and began regularly featuring translations of Afro-Asian writers, African American writers and Latin American writers, moving away from its earlier emphasis on Soviet and western authors (Liu 2014: 166). This reality of an emerging new literary world order was clearly not lost on the participating writers in the AWC, who saw in translation a huge potential for cultural dialogue amongst the Asian writers as well as for giving Asian literature its due place within world literature, a task that would get a major impetus encompassing Africa too after the First Afro-Asian Writers' Conference in Tashkent in October 1958, when translation would become a major platform for reinventing and expanding the canon of world literature. Hala Halim, through her archival research on *Lotus* (Halim 2012, 2020), the trilingual quarterly journal of the Afro-Asian Writers' Association launched in 1968, has detailed how the journal created transnational literary bridges, particularly across Asia and Africa, but also Latin America, and how, by the very fact of its publication in Arabic in addition to English and French, *Lotus* had at its core an autonomous translational project of the Third World that was not mediated by the West:

> Of foremost importance to the Afro-Asian nexus as a case study of Global South comparatism is the question of language, and hence translation. The "literature of riposte" and of "the empire writing back," which is one dominant model in Western postcolonial criticism, with its attendant an-glophone and francophone literatures, while it commands a measure of descriptive purchase, retains for the empire a centrality that in reality was contested in the solidarities of Bandung and associated movements.
>
> (Halim 2012: 571)[13]

It is in this context that the translation of Bhabani Bhattacharya's novel *He Who Rides the Tiger* by Miguel Ángel Asturias and Blanca Mora needs to be placed. A writer and diplomat, like Asturias himself, Bhattacharya is one of the leading figures of Indian Writing in English of the post-independence period, along with Mulk Raj Anand, R.K. Narayan, Raja Rao, Kamala Markan-day, Manohar Malgonkar and others who forged the social realist idiom of the post-independence Indo-Anglian novel. Dorothy B. Shimer, in the preface to the literary biography of Bhattacharya, tells us that his novels were simultane-ously published in India and in the United States and "moved rapidly into the stream of world literature through translations into twenty or more languages" (np). *He Who Rides a Tiger* was published in 1954, and by 1956, it had already been translated into several languages. Asturias and Blanca Mora's Spanish translation *El que cabalga un tigre* (1958), was based on the French translation done by Dominique Guillet, titled *Qui chevauche un tigre* (1956).[14]

He Who Rides a Tiger, like his first novel, *So Many Hungers!* (1947), has as its backdrop the Great Bengal Famine of 1943, in which nearly three mil-lion people died of hunger and starvation. While the colonial state ascribed the famine to natural causes – poor monsoon, inefficient food production, droughts etc. – economic historians such as Amartya Sen in *Poverty and Famines* have demonstrated how colonial policies were the cause of the disaster (Sen 1981: 58–85). With its focus on hunger, poverty, exploitation and sexual violence, *He Who Rides a Tiger* has therefore, quite rightly, been considered "an epistemological alternative to imperial narratives about the famine" (Sinha 2020: 69). In a journalistic piece written on the novel, published in the Spanish daily *ABC* (December 29, 1969), Miguel Ángel Asturias calls it "un grito de protesta por el hambre y la penuria que sufre el pueblo hindú" [a cry of protest against the hunger and penury that the Indian people suffer]. Imbued with the spirit of the freedom struggle and of the Quit India Movement of 1942, Bhattacharya's novel carries an anti-imperialist impulse, which one also finds in many of Miguel Ángel Asturias's novels, particularly in his works of the 1950s and 1960s, such as those that comprise the banana trilogy, set against the backdrop of the banana plantation economy in Guatemala and the role of the United Fruit Company. However, what is emphasized in this brief article by Asturias is how the novel, while indicting the colonial regime as the political cause of the famine, is equally an indictment of the superstition and the scourge of the caste system, which dominate the Indian psyche. Asturias corroborates this condition through his own observations during his stay in India and concludes that *He Who Rides the Tiger* "es una novela reveladora de una serie de situaciones que nadie se atreve a denunciar" [is a novel revealing a series of situations that no one dares to denounce] (Asturias, *ABC* 1969). A comparison of Miguel Ángel Asturias own novels, especially those of the banana trilogy, with Bhattacharya's famine novels would yield interesting insights into the narrative strategies these writers employ to capture the ravages of the modernizing impulse under colonialism and neo-colonialism while recording at the same time experiences of race and caste-based exploitation in their respective societies.

Finally, Miguel Ángel Asturias's visit to India and his participation in the AWC were not a chance encounter and have to be seen in the context of the Nehruvian state's endeavour at crafting out modern independent India's international linkages in the arena of culture. The nascent nation state was actively developing institutional structures and intellectual networks. In the 1950s and 1960s, quite a few Latin American writers and artists travelled to India, some invited by the Indian government, as was the case with Miguel Ángel Asturias or David Alfaro Siqueiros, the Mexican muralist, who also visited India in the same year as Asturias on Jawaharlal Nehru's invitation and others, like Julio Cortázar, Jorge Zalamea and Octavio Paz who spent time in India around these years for diverse reasons and have left an important body of writing on India. Miguel Ángel Asturias's chronicles on India continue the stirrings of transregional anti-imperialist solidarity already present in Latin American modernists of the end of the 19th century such as José Martí and later in the avant-garde writers, one of whom, Asturias's contemporary, the Peruvian José Carlos Mariátegui, has been discussed in the previous chapter. Retrieving from oblivion Asturias's visit to India and the texts he wrote is to build on this historical memory of tricontinentalism for contemporary Global South solidarity.

Notes

1 The translation from the original poem in Spanish is by us.
2 The Latin American *crónica* or the chronicle is a genre midway between journalism and literature. These are short texts published in newspapers and offer a vignette of urban life, customs, or events. It has been a constant in Latin American literature, changing its function and role with the times.
3 Mariátegui's texts on India are dispersed through his writings. The texts on Mahatma Gandhi and Rabindranath Tagore form part of a long essay titled "El mensaje del Oriente" [The Message from the Orient] (Mariategui 1997: 107–122) originally published in 1925. Other essays – "El movimiento nacionalista hindú" [Indian National Movement] (Mariátegui 1997: 157–158), "La lucha en la India por la independencia nacional" [India's Struggle for National Independence] (Mariátegui 1997: 181–183) and "Los votos del Congreso Nacional Hindú" [The Declarations of the Indian National Congress] (Mariátegui 1997: 184–185) were originally published in various journals between 1929 and 1930.
4 This is not to say that Latin America had not earlier been a part of transnational anti-imperialist networks. Several Latin American delegates had participated in the 1927 "International Congress against Colonial Oppression and Imperialism" held in Brussels. Even before that, the Anti-Imperialist League of the Americas (LADLA), had been founded in Mexico in 1924 (Obregon). Anne Garland Mahler, in her recent study (2022), sees LADLA as the foundation of Latin American engagement with Afro-Asian anti-colonialism (47) and considers OSPAAL not so much an offshoot of Bandung as is commonly held in current scholarship, but as drawing from the historical memory of the LADLA (44).
5 The trilogy comprises *Viento fuerte* (1950) [*Strong Wind*; Translated by Gregory Rabassa, New York: Delacorte Press, 1969]; *El Papa Verde* (1954) [*The Green Pope*; Translated by Gregory Rabassa, New York: Delacorte Press, 1971]; *Los ojos de los enterrados* (1960) [*The Eyes of the Interred;* Translated by Gregory Rabassa, New York: Delacorte Press, 1973]. These three novels depict the exploitation that the Guatemalan peasants suffered in the banana plantations owned by the United Fruit Company and are emblematic of the socially committed fiction of Asturias.
6 Known as the "Peoples' Bandung," the Conference of Asian Countries on the Relaxation of International Tension (CRIT) was a non-governmental initiative. Stolte (2019) highlights the importance of this and other similar mass-based initiatives beyond the interstate Afro-Asian solidarity represented by the Bandung Conference.
7 These preparatory meetings for the AWC in Delhi were attended by delegates from Burma, China, Korea, Nepal and Vietnam, and the host country India. Dr. Mulk Raj Anand, the convener of the conference, was one of the founding members of the All India Progressive Writers' Association, though Indian delegates represented all hues of the ideological spectrum.
8 It is not a coincidence that the First International Congress of Black Writers and Artists, was held around the same time (from September 19–22, 1956) at the Sorbonne in Paris. As a platform for leading Black intellectuals of the time, this Congress has been considered a landmark event in Black internationalism. Interestingly, the poster for this Congress was made by Pablo Picasso. For more on this Congress, see Frioux-Salgas (2021).
9 Blanca Mora y Araujo, in her memoir, recalls the visit to China as well as India at length. A detailed account of Latin American authors and artists who visited China in the 1950s is available in Rothwell (2013).
10 All excerpts cited from the chronicles of Miguel Ángel Asturias have been translated by the authors.
11 All references to the AWC reports, unless otherwise mentioned, have been cited from the Natarang Pratishthan archival holdings on the Asian Writers' Conference.

12 In her memoir, Blanca Mora recalls their journeys together by train. Zalamea wrote his famous *El sueño de las escalinatas* (1964) around this time that he spent in India.
13 Halim also mentions that there have been efforts in Cairo towards reactivating the Afro-Asian Writers' Association and reconstituting it by including Latin America and calling it the Association of the South (2012: 566).
14 The translation must have been undertaken by the Asturias couple soon after their return to Paris in early 1957 for it to have been published in 1958. Other novels of Bhabani Bhattacharya translated into Spanish are *A Goddess Named Gold* (1960) [*Una diosa llamada oro*. Barcelona: Editorial Vergara (1962) translated from English by Irene Orus Hostench]; *Music for Mohini* (1952) [*Música para Mohini*. Barcelona: Editorial Vergara (1963)].

References

Alonso, I. H. (2017). M.N. Roy and the Mexican Revolution: How a Militant Indian Nationalist Became an International Communist. *South Asia: Journal of South Asian Studies*, 40 (3), 517–530.

Asian-African Conference (1955). Final Communique. In *Asia-Africa Speak From Bandung*. Jakarta: Ministry of Foreign Affairs, 161–169. Retrieved from: www.cvce.eu/en/obj/final_communique_of_the_asian_african_conference_of_bandung_24_april_1955-en-676237bd-72f7-471f-949a-88b6ae513585.html [Viewed 12/01/2022]

Asturias, M. A. (1946). *El Señor Presidente*. Mexico City: Costa Amic.

Asturias, M. A. (1969). El que cabalga un tigre. *ABC*, https://www.abc.es/archivo/periodicos/abc-madrid-19691221.html [Viewed 12/01/2022].

Asturias, M. A. (1981). *Viajes, Ensayos y Fantasías*. Prologue and Compilation by Richard J. Callan. Buenos Aires: Losada.

Bellini, G. (1999). *Mundo mágico y el mundo real: la narrativa de Miguel Ángel Asturias*. Buenos Aires: Losada.

Bergel, M. (2015). *El Oriente desplazado: los intelectuales y el origen del tercermundismo en la Argentina*. Bernal: Universidad Nacional de Quilmes.

Bhattacharya, B. (1954). *He Who Rides a Tiger*. New York: Crown Publishers.

Bhattacharya, B. (1956). *Qui chevauche un tigre*. Translation into French by D. Guillet. Paris: Calmann-Lévy.

Bhattacharya, B. (1947). *So Many Hungers!*. Bombay: Hind Kitab.

Bhattacharya, B. (1958). *El que cabalga un tigre*. Translation into Spanish by M. Ángel Asturias and B. Mora de Araujo. Buenos Aires: Goyanarte.

Bolívar, S., Fornoff, F. H. and Bushnell, D. (2003). *El Libertador: Writings of Simón Bolívar*. Oxford: Oxford University Press.

Bose, S. and Pande, I. (2011). Tagorean Universalism and Cosmopolitanism. *India International Centre Quarterly* Vol. 38, No. 1, 2–17.

Civantos, C. (2005). *Between Argentines and Arabs: Argentine Orientalism, Arab Immigrants, and the Writing of Identity*. Albany, NY: SUNY University Press.

Cunha, A. M., and Britto, G. (2017). When Development Meets Culture: The Contribution of Celso Furtado in the 1970s. *Cambridge Journal of Economics*, 1–22. https://doi.org/10.1093/cje/bex021

Desai, M. V. (1957). The Asian Writers' Conference December 1956: New Delhi. *Books Abroad*, 31 (3), 243–245.

Devés Valdés, E. and Melgar Bao, R (2007). Redes teosóficas y pensadores (políticos) latinoamericanos, 1910–1930. In E. Devés Valdés (Ed.), *Redes intelectuales en América Latina. Hacia la constitución de una comunidad intelectual.* Santiago: IDEA/Universidad de Santiago de Chile, 75–92.

Djagalov, R. (2019). Progress Publishers: A Short History. In V. Prashad (Ed.), *The East Was Read: Socialist Culture in the Third World.* New Delhi: Leftword, 78–86.

Dussel, E. D. (1997). *The Invention of the Americas: Eclipse of "the Other" and the Myth of Modernity.* New York: Continuum Press.

Frioux-Salgas, S. (2021). Le 1er Congrès International des écrivains et artistes noirs (Paris, Sorbonne, 19–22 septembre 1956): Replay. *Hommes & Migrations,* 1332, 143–149.

Gleijeses, P. (1991). *Shattered Hope: The Guatemalan Revolution and the United States (1944–1954).* Princeton, NJ: Princeton University Press.

Goebel, M. (2014). Geopolitics, Transnational Solidarity or Diaspora Nationalism? The Global Career of MN Roy, 1915–1930. *European Review of History: Revue européenne d'histoire,* 21 (4), 485–499.

Guillén, N. (1973). *Tengo.* Havana: Consejo Nacional de Cultura.

Gupta, S. S. (2019). Intersubaltern Dialogue or Reworked Essentialisms? Kabir's Translations into Spanish in Latin America. *International Journal of European Languages,* 1 (1), 90–107.

Halim, H. (2012). *Lotus,* the Afro-Asian Nexus, and Global South Comparatism. *Comparative Studies of South Asia, Africa, and the Middle East,* 32 (3), 563–583.

Halim, H.(2019a). *Afro-Asian Third-Worldism Into Global South: The Case of Lotus Journal. Global South Studies: A Collective Publication with The Global South.* Retrieved from: https://globalsouthstudies.as.virginia.edu/ key-moments/afro-asian-third-worldism-global-south-case-lotus-journal [Viewed 30/10/2021]

Halim, H. (2019b). The Pre-postcolonial and its Enduring Relevance: Afro-Asian Variations in Edwar al-Kharrat's Texts. In *Postcolonialism Cross-Examined: Multidirectional Perspectives on Imperial and Colonial Pasts and the Neocolonial Present.* London: Routledge, 79–95.

Halim H. (2020). Translating Solidarity: An Interview with Nehad Salem. *Critical Times,* 3 (1), 131–147.

Han, G. B. (2018). Nazim Hikmet's Afro-Asian solidarities. *Safundi,* 19 (3), 284–305.

Harlow, B. (1987). *Resistance Literature.* New York: Methuen Press.

Jansen, H. (2019). Soviet 'Afro-Asians' in UNESCO: Reorienting World History. *Journal of World History,* 30 (1–2), 193–221.

Jia, Y. (2019). Beyond the "Bhai-Bhai" Rhetoric: China-India Literary Relations, 1950–1990. PhD Thesis, SOAS, University of London. Retrieved from: http://eprints.soas.ac.uk/32203 [Viewed 31/08/2021]

Jia, Y. (2021). Cultural Bandung or Writerly Cold War? Revisiting the Asian Writers' Conference from an India-China Perspective. In K. Bystrom, M. Popescu, and K. Zien (Eds.), *The Cultural Cold War and the Global South.* New York and Abingdon: Routledge, 29–44.

Kothari, R. (2018). *A Multilingual Nation: Translation and Language Dynamic in India.* New Delhi: Oxford University Press.

Lenin, V. I. (1974). *Imperialism, the Highest Stage of Capitalism, Lenin Collected Works,* Vol. 22. Moscow: Progress Publishers. https://www.marxists.org/archive/lenin/works/cw/pdf/lenin-cw-vol-22.pdf) (Viewed on August 26, 2023).

Liu, L. H. (2014). The Eventfulness of Translation: Temporality, Difference and Competing Universals. *Translation,* 4, 147–170.

Mahler, A. (2022). Global Solidarity before the Tricontinental Conference: Latin America and the League against Imperialism. In R. Parrott, and M. Lawrence (Eds.), *The Tricontinental Revolution: Third World Radicalism and the Cold War* (Cambridge Studies in US Foreign Relations). Cambridge: Cambridge University Press, 43–68.

Mangalagiri, A. (2021). A Poetics of the Writers' Conference: Literary Relation in the Cold War World. *Comparative Literature Studies*, 58 (3), 509–531.

Martí, J. (1891). Nuestra América. *La Revista Ilustrada de Nueva York*. Available at https://bibliotecavirtual.clacso.org.ar/ar/libros/osal/osal27/14Marti.pdf (Viewed on August 26, 2023).

Mariátegui, J. (1997). *José Carlos Mariátegui y el continente asiático*. Lima: Clenala.

Mora y Araujo de Asturias, B. (2017). *Memorias de mi memoria*. Guatemala: Editorial Cultura.

Panagariya, A. (2008). *India: The Emerging Giant*. New York: Oxford University Press.

Paz, O. (1995). *Vislumbres de la India*. Barcelona: Seix Barral.

Prashad, V. (Ed.) (2019). Introduction. In *The East Was Read: Socialist Culture in the Third World*. New Delhi: Leftword, 7–15.

Rothwell, M. D. (2013). *Transpacific Revolutionaries: The Chinese Revolution in Latin America*. New York and London: Routledge.

Sen, A. (1981). *Poverty and Famines: An Essay on Entitlement and Deprivation*. New York: Oxford University Press.

Sinha, B. (2020). Trauma and Referentiality in Bhabani Bhattacharya's Famine Novels. *Cultural Dynamics*, 32 (1–2), 68–81.

Stolte, C. (2019). "The People's Bandung": Local Anti-imperialists on an Afro-Asian Stage. *Journal of World History*, 30 (1–2), 125–156.

Torres-Rodriguez, L. J. (2015). Orientalizing Mexico: *Estudios indostánicos* and the Place of India in José Vasconcelos's *La raza cósmica*. *Revista Hispánica Moderna*, 68 (1), 77–91. Retrieved from: www.jstor.org/stable/90024970

Uchmany, E. A. (2003). *India-Mexico: Similarities and Encounters Throughout History*. New Delhi: Indian Council of Cultural Relations.

Villamar, C. (2021). *Portuguese Merchants in the Manila Galleon System (1565–1600)*. London and New York: Routledge.

Vogeley, N. (1995). Turks and Indians: Orientalist Discourse in Postcolonial Mexico. *Diacritics*, 25 (1), 3–20.

Washbourne, K. (2011). 'The Nightmare Man Is Weaving Tales': Translator's Introduction. In M. A. Asturias, *Legends of Guatemala*. Translated by K. Washbourne. Pittsburgh, PA: Latin American Literary Review Press, 13–42.

Ya, H. S. (1956). Report presented by the Korean Delegation in the AWC, AWC File, Natarang Pratishthan Archives, Delhi NCR.

Yoon, D. M. (2012). The Global South and Cultural Struggles: On the Afro-Asian People's Solidarity Organization. *Journal of Contemporary Thought*, 35, 40–46.

Yoon, D. M. (2015). 'Our Forces Have Redoubled': World Literature, Postcolonialism, and the Afro-Asian Writers' Bureau. *Cambridge Journal of Postcolonial Literary Inquiry*, 2 (2), 233–252.

Yoon, D. M. (2018). Bandung Nostalgia and the Global South. In R. West-Pavlov (Ed.), *The Global South and Literature* (Cambridge Critical Concepts). Cambridge: Cambridge University Press, 23–33.

Young, R. (2005). Postcolonialism: From Bandung to the Tricontinental. *Historein*, 5, 11–21.

Zalamea, J. (1964) *El sueño de las escalinatas*. Bogota: Tercer Mundo.

Zavala, I. M. (1992). *Colonialism and Culture: Hispanic Modernisms and the Social Imaginary*. Bloomington: Indiana University Press.

Conclusion

The preceding chapters draw on the writings of literary figures, political activists and policymakers. They deal with a wide variety of themes, ranging from the challenges of underdevelopment to the politics of the world literary order. Underlying this diversity are three common themes that run through the pages of this book, which roughly covers the period from the mid-19th to the mid-20th centuries. This is first and foremost a book about the dynamics of development and the multiple ways in which it has been theorized in India and Latin America, seen through a relational and connected framework. Chapter 1, for example draws attention to the writings of Dadabhai Naoroji and Raúl Prebisch on the intricate connections between imperialism and underdevelopment. In contrast to much of the Western development discourse, which has conceptualized capitalism as a closed system, both of these thinkers brought out in sharp contrast the determining role of global asymmetries in shaping patterns of accumulation in peripheral regions. From the dynamics of global unequal exchange, Chapter 2 shifts focus to the complex interconnections between social oppression, class and capitalism. Traditionally, caste, gender and race-based oppressions have remained invisible to the development discourse and the little work that has emerged has tended to divorce social oppression from the nature of capitalist development. Social oppression has come to be seen as a problem stemming from stymied/compressed/incomplete capitalist development rather than a direct outgrowth of its exploitative logic (Mosse 2018, Jodhka 2016). Chapter 2 challenges this perspective by drawing on the writings of B.R. Ambedkar and José Carlos Mariátegui. It reflects on the modernity of social oppression and points to the centrality of anti-racism and anti-casteism in emancipatory movements. Finally, Chapter 3 focuses on the decolonial experimentations of Miguel Ángel Asturias by drawing on his travel chronicles in India. These chronicles, we argue, have to be seen as part of a sweeping wave of decolonial cosmopolitanism that engulfed Latin America and India in the early and mid-20th centuries. Asturias's writings reflect a profound sense of solidarity with a country devastated by colonialism, even as he beamed in admiration of its literary, technological and economic achievements. His travel writings show that he came to see Nehruvian developmentalism as the

DOI: 10.4324/9781003316084-5

assertion of self-determination in the economic arena and as an important counterpart to struggles against cultural dominance in the West. Today, of course, the entire idea of national self-determination has come to be seen as a subject that is passé, and the viability of state-led development has all but been dismissed by social theory. In its place, laissez-faire, neoliberal and post-development discourses have come to dominate discussions. Asturias's writings, born as they were in the cauldron of anti-imperialist struggles and rising tides of decolonial cosmopolitanism, are important correctives to these reductive interpretations and point to the need for more nuanced perspectives on national sovereignty, the nation-state and development.

A second and equally important thread that runs through the book is the recurrent theme of connections. The intellectuals that this book surveys shared common anti-imperialist visions and were driven by a fervent search for civilizational models beyond the West. But what our comparative and relational intellectual history also reveals is that their most innovative attempts at decolonizing epistemology were driven not so much by a desire to turn inwards and break away from Western canons as much as they were aimed at challenging the imperial project of parcelling knowledge into graded, discrete boxes. All the thinkers that this book has surveyed were heavily influenced by enlightenment thought, especially Marxism, and yet, in their own ways, each contributed to tearing down Eurocentric narratives. The most influential thinkers of the South sought to build bridges and reconstruct connections, asserting difference without losing sight of what is common and shared. These transmodern yearnings reveal intriguing avenues of collaboration and convergence that are often missed in today's polarized academic debates (Rathore and Verma 2011; Salem 2019; Krishnaswamy 2022). To be sure, influential streams within the decolonial framework have implicated Western thought in the destruction of Southern knowledge systems, and in turn, leading European thinkers have tended to dismiss decolonial critiques in the name of upholding an idealized notion of universalism (Mignolo 2011; Grosfoguel 2012; De Sousa Santos 2018; Žižek 1998). Yet between the bland universalism being peddled by the votaries of Eurocentrism and the reductive post-colonial emphasis on difference, there lies a vast space where new alliances and productive dialogues are possible. This is particularly true of Marxism. While influential decolonial scholars have tended to paint Marx as a racist and have thus relegated any discourse that is even distinctly Marxist as fruit from the poisoned tree, the historical fact remains that Marxism has remained a central rallying point for emancipatory movements in much of the non-West, from China to Cuba and elsewhere. To dismiss Marxism as part and parcel of Eurocentric theory is to miss its journey from European heartlands to its Eastern peripheries and finally onto the Southern world; a journey, one might add, that involved constant reconstruction, innovation and creative incorporation into local contexts (Salem 2019).

Lastly, the thinkers and writers dealt with in this book are not relics from the past. They wrote at a time that was very different from our own, and their immediate social and political contexts weighed heavily on their works. That said, this book suggests that the thinkers from these two regions have abiding relevance in the world that we live in today as well. The protests that were sparked after the police killings of George Floyd and Breonna Taylor in 2020 were a grim reminder of the continued sway of racism in contemporary societies. The debates that emerged in the wake of these killings renewed attention to the historical and contemporary role of unequal exchange and imperialism in shaping capitalist development (Bhattacharyya 2018; Roediger 2019; Singh 2016, 2017; Obeng-Odoom 2020; Smith 2016; Patnaik and Patnaik 2021). There have of course been several rich discussions on imperialism, slavery and the racial basis of capitalism in the past as well, but these have largely remained on the side-lines of the development field, despite some notable exceptions. Revisiting the writings of thinkers from India and Latin America can serve as a useful starting point to think through these issues. This book, we hope, can add to the ongoing efforts to widen the scope of academic debates.

References

Bhattacharyya, G. (2018). *Rethinking Racial Capitalism: Questions of Reproduction and Survival*. London: Rowman & Littlefield.

De Sousa Santos, B. (2018). *The End of the Cognitive Empire. The Coming of Age of Epistemologies of the South*. London: Duke University Press.

Grosfoguel, R. (2012). Decolonizing Western Uni-versalisms: Decolonial Pluri-versalism from Aimé Césaire to the Zapatistas. *Transmodernity: Journal of Peripheral Cultural Production of the Luso-Hispanic World*, 1 (3).

Jodhka, S. S. (2016). Ascriptive Hierarchies: Caste and Its Reproduction in Contemporary India. *Current Sociology*, 64 (2), 228–243.

Krishnaswamy, R. (2022). Transmodern Liberation Philosophies: B.R. Ambedkar and Enrique Dussel. *Interventions*, 24 (8), 1212–1228. https://doi.org/10.1080/13698 01X.2021.2003222

Mignolo, W. D. (2011). Geopolitics of Sensing and Knowing: On (de) Coloniality, Border Thinking and Epistemic Disobedience. *Postcolonial Studies*, 14 (3), 273–283.

Mosse, D. (2018). Caste and Development: Contemporary Perspectives on a Structure of Discrimination and Advantage. *World Development*, 110, 422–436.

Obeng-Odoom, F. (2020). *Property, Institutions, and Social Stratification in Africa*. Cambridge: Cambridge University Press.

Patnaik, U. and Patnaik, P. (2021). *Capital and Imperialism: Theory, History, and the Present*. New York: Monthly Review Press.

Rathore, A. S. and Verma, A. (2011). Editors' Introduction. In *B. R. Ambedkar: The Buddha and His Dhamma, A Critical Edition*. Oxford: Oxford University Press, ix–xxiv.

Roediger, D. R. (2019). *Class, Race, and Marxism*. New York: Verso Books.

Salem, S. (2019). 'Stretching' Marxism in the Postcolonial World: Egyptian Decolonisation and the Contradictions of National Sovereignty. *Historical Materialism*, 27 (4), 3–28.

Singh, N. P. (2016). On Race, Violence, and So-Called Primitive Accumulation. *Social Text*, 34 (3), 27–50.

Singh, N. P. (2017). *Race and America's Long War*. Berkeley: University of California Press.

Smith, J. (2016). *Imperialism in the Twenty-First Century: Globalization, Super-Exploitation, and Capitalism's Final Crisis*. New York: New York University press.

Žižek, S. (1998). A Leftist plea for "Eurocentrism". *Critical Inquiry*, 24 (4), 988–1009.

Index

For Product Safety Concerns and Information please contact our EU
representative GPSR@taylorandfrancis.com
Taylor & Francis Verlag GmbH, Kaufingerstraße 24, 80331 München, Germany

www.ingramcontent.com/pod-product-compliance
Lightning Source LLC
Chambersburg PA
CBHW061837220326
41599CB00027B/5308

* 9 7 8 1 0 3 2 3 2 6 6 0 3 *